everyday
Salads

everyday
Salads

MURDOCH
BOOKS

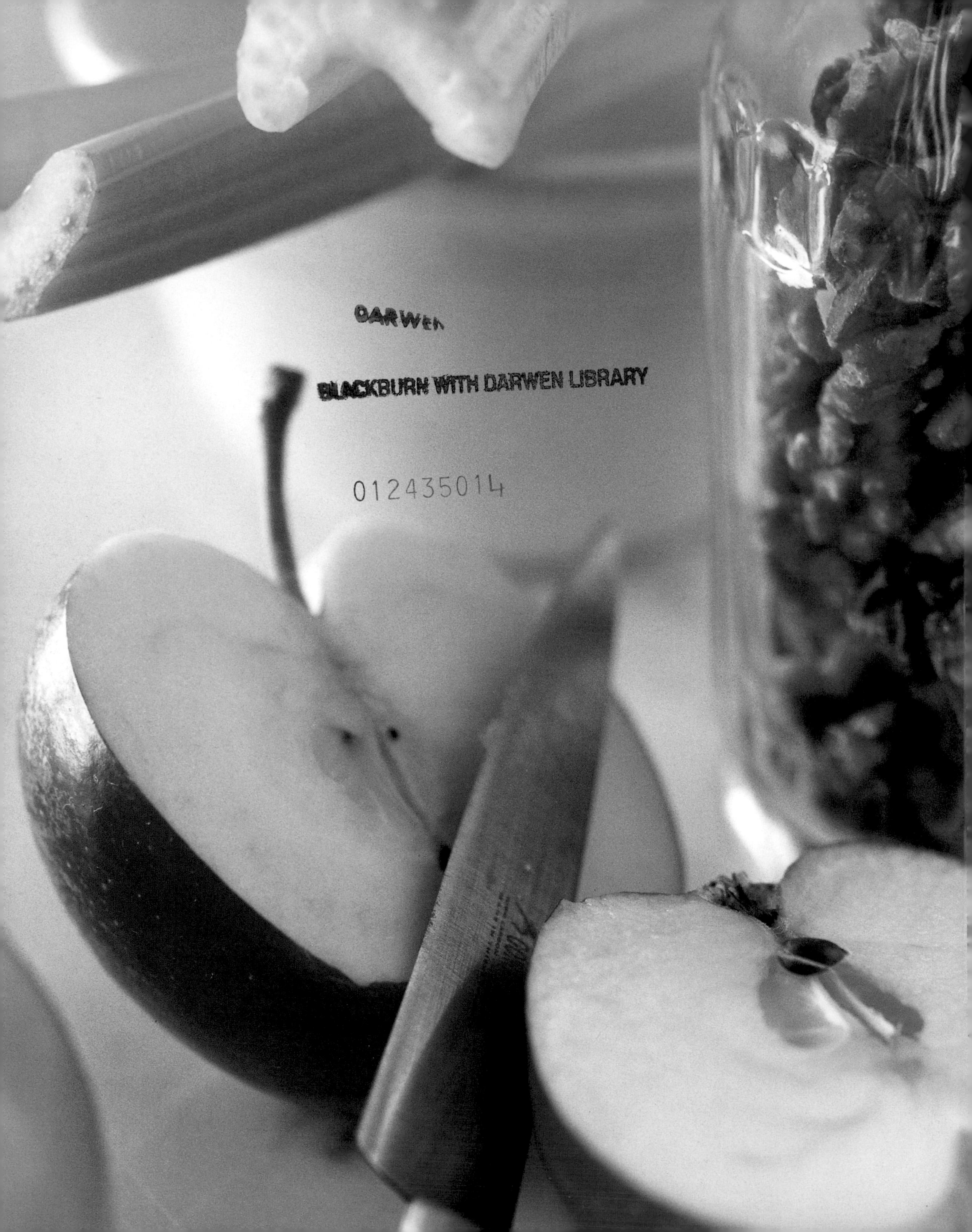

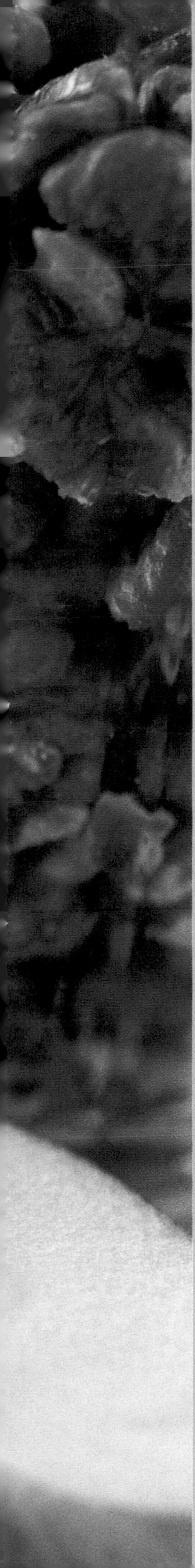

contents

vegetable basics 6

glossary of salad greens 10

classics 12

starters & sides 38

main meal salads 64

low fat 114

vinaigrettes & dressings 148

mayonnaise 150

glossary 152

index 153

Vegetable Basics

Our markets and supermarkets are overflowing with delicious and healthy vegetables. This guide to purchasing, storing, cooking and presentation will help you prepare successful and delicious vegetable dishes.

Vegetables picked fresh from the garden are still the best but, as most of us do not have a vegetable garden to harvest, we turn to the local greengrocer or supermarket. And there, thanks to modern methods of cold storage and transportation, we find vegetables available to us year-round that a couple of years ago were only on sale for a few short weeks. The sheer abundance and variety of vegetables, whether fresh, frozen or packaged, means that the days of meals featuring boring, boiled vegetables are banished forever.

This book brings together all the basic methods of storing, preparing and cooking vegetables to retain their colour, flavour and nutrients, plus recipes from many nations. For the adventurous cook, Asian food stores and vegetable markets are full of delicious ingredients, all quite simple to prepare.

PURCHASING

Little and often is a good maxim to follow when shopping for vegetables. Always buy vegetables that look fresh and crisp and have a bright natural colour. Buying fresh vegetables in season is economical, and means you get the best flavour because of the short storage time.

If you have a definite vegetable recipe in mind, but can only find sad-looking specimens of the one you require, find a substitute (e.g. canned tomatoes or frozen spinach) or buy another vegetable that looks in peak condition, and save your first choice until you can find a fresh supply.

Freshness is important, especially in green leafy vegetables with a high water content, such as lettuces and spinach, because vitamin losses begin soon after picking.

Many vegetables are available ready-packed in net or plastic bags, or sometimes polystyrene trays, in convenient amounts. Before buying these, check that the produce is fresh and undamaged.

Roots and tubers—carrots, potatoes, parsnip, beetroots, turnips—should be unblemished, with no musty smell. Loose, unwashed potatoes are a better buy than washed and packaged ones; you can pick them over for size and quality, while the earth around the potato keeps it in good condition. Don't buy any that are sprouting or have a green tinge.

Onions, white, red or brown, are at their 'sweetest' when their tops are still green, but you won't find them like that in the shops, as they are picked when their tops have shrivelled to

allow maximum growth. Choose those with smooth skins and no dark or damp patches.

The Brassica family (all types of cabbage, Brussels sprouts, broccoli and cauliflower) should have crisp leaves; cabbages should be tightly packed and heavy; cauliflowers should be white or creamy-white, without any discoloured patches. Broccoli should have firm, tight, dark green florets, not yellowed or loose-looking; avoid any that have flowered.

Buy eggplant (aubergine) that are firm, with shiny smooth purple skin; capsicum (pepper) (particularly check the red ones) and cucumbers should be crisp and quite hard, with no wrinkled skin or mushy patches—if in doubt, squeeze gently.

Tomatoes can be purchased ripe or not, according to your preference and how they are to be used. Whether you are buying large meaty types or tiny cherry tomatoes choose the reddest you can find, as firm or soft as you need (vine ripened have the best flavour). Leave firm tomatoes to ripen at room temperature. Keep in mind that canned tomatoes are perfect for many dishes.

Legumes (green beans, broad/fava beans, etc, and peas, sugar snap peas and snow peas/mangetouts) should

To store mushrooms, wipe over with paper towels or a damp cloth.

Place into a brown paper bag and refrigerate for up to three days.

To prepare asparagus, break off the hard ends and discard.

be bright green and have no wrinkles in the skin. Smaller specimens are younger and therefore more tender. They should 'snap' rather than bend when broken.

Sweet corn is also best when young. This summer treat should be delicious enough to eat raw, but usually has become a little too tough by the time it reaches the shelf. Choose cobs with unblemished husks. Pull the husks back to check that the kernels are even-sized, small and tender, and that there are no caterpillars lurking. Dented-looking kernels mean the corn is not fresh and will be tough when cooked.

Freshness is particularly important with salad vegetables. Don't buy green vegetables that are wilted, dry-looking or have yellow or brown patches or insect-nibbled leaves. Crisp-head lettuces (iceberg, cos/romaine) should feel firm when squeezed and the base should be dry. Many loose-head lettuces are sold with their roots intact; this helps to keep them in good condition.

Stalky vegetables, such as celery, fennel and asparagus, should be crisp and firm with no brown patches. Celery should be heavy and stand up straight, with light green leaves. Fennel should be white and crunchy.

When buying asparagus, choose straight even-sized stalks with tight buds—thick stalks are more tender than thin. The cut end should be dry but not withered.

Artichokes should have silky, compact green heads with no dark patches.

Choose avocados according to what you are using them for. For example,

you may want a really ripe one to purée, a perfect one to eat immediately or a firmer one to keep. Press gently to test for ripeness; the flesh should just give at the stem end. Avoid those with bruised or black/brown patches. Place hard avocados in a brown paper bag and put in a warm place (e.g. on top of the refrigerator, at the back over the motor) to ripen in two days.

Bunches of fresh green herbs such as parsley, chives and basil are best kept in water in the shop, and should look and smell freshly picked.

STORING

Shopping frequently for vegetables means that you can take advantage of what looks best on the day, but unfortunately this is not always practical. Shopping weekly means that you must store your vegetables carefully to retain maximum flavour and vitamins.

Most vegetables benefit from being stored in a cool, dark place. Generally, vegetables keep best when stored in the crisper section of the refrigerator. Store them unwashed and loosely packed in plastic bags. Squeeze the air out of the bags before storing. Fresh ginger can be refrigerated unwrapped.

Leafy green vegetables such as lettuce and spinach should be washed and thoroughly dried by spinning or patting dry with a tea towel or paper towels. (Water leaches out vitamins from the leaves.) Hit the base of the lettuce hard on a bench or board to loosen the core, then turn over and twist it out. Pack whole lettuce or leaves loosely in plastic bags. Squeeze air out of the bag, seal and place in

the crisper section of the refrigerator. Properly stored, lettuces will last up to seven days for crisphead and two to three days for soft butter types.

Mushrooms can be stored in the refrigerator, but should be wiped clean and placed in a brown paper bag. This way they will keep in good condition for three to four days. Do not store them in plastic because they will begin to decay quickly.

Potatoes should not be refrigerated as they can develop a sweetish taste. To store, remove from plastic bags and place in a hessian or paper bag. Keep them in a cool, dark, dry place with good ventilation. Properly stored, they should remain in good condition for two months or more. Sweet potatoes, turnips, onions (except for spring onions/scallions) and garlic should be stored in the same manner.

For convenience, both raw garlic and ginger can be puréed in a food processor or blender and stored in glass jars in the refrigerator.

Tomatoes are a subtropical crop and low temperatures damage their cell structure, so they should not be refrigerated. The optimum storage temperature for tomatoes is 10°C (50°F), but keeping them at room temperature until needed is the most convenient for most cooks, and underripe fruit will ripen best at room temperature. Take tomatoes out of plastic bags to avoid the growth of bacteria. Keep them away from sunlight—it destroys vitamin C. Store in a single layer unless you want the tomatoes to ripen quickly, as heat rather than light causes ripening. Remove any tomatoes that have spoilt.

Trim any remaining woody ends with a vegetable peeler.

To store lettuce, wash, dry and loosen core by hitting on a bench or board.

Turn the lettuce over and twist out the core. Wrap and refrigerate.

FREEZING

Most fresh vegetables are not suitable to freeze raw, but many can be blanched, then successfully frozen. Blanched asparagus spears, beans, broccoli, carrots, cauliflower, corn (whole cobs or kernels), shelled peas and skinned tomatoes all freeze well. Freezing is a good way to take advantage of a seasonal glut in produce.

Pick over and discard any damaged specimens. Wash and cut the vegetable into pieces as desired. Plunge into boiling water for 30 seconds, then into iced water to refresh. Pat dry with paper towels, pack into freezer bags, expel air and seal. Label and freeze. Frozen blanched vegetables will keep for up to three months.

Fresh herbs can be successfully frozen. Wash and dry the leaves, place into small freezer bags, expel air and seal. Label and freeze.

To freeze cooked vegetable dishes, stock, purées, soups and sauces, cool the just-cooked dish quickly, place in plastic containers, seal, label and freeze. As a general rule, freeze for up to two months.

Commercial or home-frozen vegetables should be added to recipes unthawed, and toward the end of the cooking time.

Stocks, sauces and precooked dishes should be thawed in the refrigerator and reheated gently before serving.

PREPARING

Before cooking, wash vegetables well to remove any pesticide residue, as well as grit or insects. Leeks, spinach and silverbeet (Swiss chard)

To salt eggplant (aubergine), place it in a colander, sprinkle over salt.

need to be washed thoroughly to remove sand.

Some vegetables require particular techniques to cook and present them at their best. The following methods are frequently used in this book.

Salting. Salting is used when cooking eggplant (aubergine) and large zucchini (courgette) or cucumbers, to draw out excess moisture and any bitterness from the vegetable. Salting eggplant slices before frying will cut the amount of oil needed by two-thirds. To salt vegetables, chop or slice according to the recipe. Place in a large colander or spread on paper towels and sprinkle with salt. Leave for at least 30 minutes, rinse under cold water, drain and pat dry with paper towels.

To peel tomatoes, make a small cross on the bottom of each tomato, and plunge into boiling water for 30 seconds. Lift out and plunge into chilled water for one minute, using plenty of water in each case. The skin can then be peeled easily from the cross using a downward motion.

To prepare artichokes, trim the stalk from base of artichoke. Using scissors,

After 30 minutes, rinse under cold water and pat dry with paper towels.

trim hard points from the outer leaves. Using a sharp knife, cut top from artichoke. Brush all cut areas with lemon juice to prevent discolouration. Cook artichokes in a stainless steel or enamel pan.

To prepare asparagus, break off the inedible woody ends and discard. If the ends are still hard, trim with a vegetable peeler.

To prepare avocado, cut the avocado in half using a sharp knife. To remove the stone, push the knife into the stone and gently twist and lift out. The skin can be peeled off with fingers.

To prepare cucumber. When seeding is called for in the recipe, peel the cucumber using a vegetable peeler (if peeling is specified), scrape out the seeds with a teaspoon and discard. Cucumbers can be given a decorative finish by peeling in stripes, or by running the tines of a fork down the outside after peeling. Use as directed.

To crush garlic cloves. Peel the garlic and place on a cutting board. Using a very sharp knife, chop the garlic finely, working in a little salt as

To peel tomatoes, make a cross cut in each tomato. Plunge into hot water.

Plunge into cold water, then peel skin down from the cut.

To chop onions, make five or six cuts through, turn and slice across.

you go. Scrape the chopped garlic together into a mound. Turn it over with the blade, chop again. Repeat until the garlic is a fine mass. For coarsely crushed garlic, press down heavily with the flat side of a wide cook's knife or cleaver. Cutting the garlic clove lengthways makes it easier to remove the skin.

To prepare mushrooms. Never peel or wash mushrooms. After wiping clean, remove stems if they are woody (reserve to make stock) and slice. Peeling and washing mushrooms removes flavour and makes them waterlogged.

To prepare onions. Peel and place on a chopping board. To chop, make five or six slices through the onion. Turn it 90°, hold layers together firmly and cut across them.

COOKING METHODS

Vegetables can be cooked in many ways, ranging from burying them in the ashes of a campfire, to combining with eggs and liqueur to make a most sophisticated soufflé.

The three cooking methods that have a particular significance for vegetables are blanching, steaming and stir-frying. These are all quick-cooking and retain all the colour, flavour and nutrition of the vegetables.

Blanching. This method is used to precook (or parboil) vegetables before adding to other cooked dishes or salads, or before freezing. The vegetables are plunged briefly into boiling water and then refreshed in cold water. This method preserves the green colour.

Steaming. Vegetables are cut into even-sized pieces and cooked in a basket or on a rack over a little boiling water or stock in a tightly covered pan. A few minutes steaming (depending on size) is enough to make green vegetables tender while remaining firm and flavourful (root vegetables take longer). This method is preferable to boiling because the flavour is

To prepare artichokes, cut off ends with a sharp knife.

preserved as the vegetable juices are not lost into the cooking water.

Stir-frying. Heat a little oil in a large frying pan or wok. Have all the vegetables cut or divided into thin even-sized pieces. Cutting celery, carrots, etc, on the diagonal gives a larger surface area and enables quicker cooking than straight sliced vegetables. When the oil is hot, add the vegetables. Toss and stir briskly around the pan for a few minutes, using a large spatula (not plastic) or spoon, over high heat. Do not let the vegetables sit still in the pan, or they will burn.

Never soak vegetables in water prior to cooking or add soda to the cooking water, as both these methods destroy vitamin C.

To remove avocado stones, place knife blade firmly into stone.

Gently twist the knife and lift out the stone.

Trim leaves with scissors and brush cut ends with lemon juice.

VEGETABLE JUICES

A quick and healthy way to make the most of vegetables is to extract the juice from them. Vegetable drinks, alone or combined with other vegetable and fruit juices make an ideal vitamin-packed pick-me-up, instant breakfast, or can be used to add extra vitamins and minerals to your diet.

Wash or peel vegetables and cut into chunks that will fit into your juice extractor. To minimize vitamin loss, cut vegetables immediately before juicing and drink the juice as soon as it is made.

Vegetables suitable for juicing are carrots, celery, tomatoes, parsley, cucumber, capsicum (pepper), cabbage, beetroot and onion. Carrot juice has a smooth and velvety texture and soothes a troubled stomach; cabbage and onion juices are reputed to help those suffering from colds; parsley, cucumber and celery juice purify the blood, while cucumber is also said to help remove cellulite.

Try these delicious juice combinations: carrot and apple; carrot, celery and apple; tomato and celery; tomato, onion and parsley; carrot, beetroot and celery.

Canned tomato juice makes the basis for an instant gazpacho: place chopped capsicum (pepper), chopped tomato, chopped cucumber, chopped celery, a little chopped onion, a crushed garlic clove and chopped parsley in food processor or blender, process until almost smooth. Stir in chilled canned tomato juice to the correct consistency. Season to taste with salt, pepper and a little lemon juice and serve. Store, covered, in refrigerator.

Glossary of Salad Greens

The best salads are made from the freshest seasonal salad leaves and herbs, tossed with a dressing to create a delicious blend of complementary flavours and textures.

SALAD LEAVES

Bok choy, also known as pak choi, is a variety of Chinese cabbage, with long white stalks and large deep-green leaves. The leaves are crisp with a sweet, cabbage-like flavour. It can be served raw or steamed.

Butter lettuce has a loosely packed head with soft leaves and a mild flavour. It is also known as butterhead.

Cabbage is crunchy and slightly sweet when served raw. The most common varieties are plain green cabbage, savoy cabbage with crinkled leaves, red cabbage (shown) and Chinese cabbage.

Chicory is a long-stemmed plant with dark-green leaves and is often combined with other greens to soften its strong, bitter flavour. It can be eaten raw, or cooked until just wilted for a milder taste.

Cos, also know as Romaine, is a large, elongated lettuce with crisp leaves and a slightly sharp flavour.

Curly Endive is frilly, with narrow prickly leaves. It has a bitter taste, the baby endive having a softer, delicate texture.

English spinach has dark-green leaves with a long thin stem and a slightly earthy flavour. It should not be confused with silverbeet, which has very large leaves. The young tender leaves are best used in salads. Baby spinach leaves are also available.

Tatsoi has dark-green leaves with thick stalks. It resembles silverbeet, but is much smaller. Sold as a whole. Also known as Rosette bok choy.

Mesclun is a combination of a variety of baby lettuce leaves and edible flowers. The type of lettuce included will vary according to the season.

Mignonette is from the same family as butter lettuce. It has thinner leaves with red-tinged edges and tends to have a smaller head than butter lettuce.

Mizuna greens have a mild mustard flavour and are best eaten raw while they are still young. The mature plants have coarser, more serrated leaves.

Radicchio is part of the chicory family. It has ruby-red leaves with fine white ribs and the slightly bitter flavour common to the chicory group.

Rocket, also known as arugula or Italian cress, has a distinct tangy, peppery flavour. The mature leaves have a much stronger flavour and are often too strong to be served on their own.

Sprouts add flavour and texture to salads and, if fresh and crisp, need no preparation. They are generally sold in punnets, and should be refrigerated and used soon after they are bought as they tend to soften after a few days. Varieties include alfalfa (top), mung bean sprouts (centre), snow pea sprouts (bottom) and bean sprouts.

Witlof, also known as Belgian endive, has smooth, creamy-white leaves with pale yellow or green tips and a slightly bitter taste. There is also a red-tipped variety.

SALAD HERBS

Basil has a unique strong scent and flavour. It is the main ingredient of pesto and is also used in dressings. Other varieties include sweet basil, purple or opal basil, bush basil and aniseed basil.

Chervil is a delicate herb with a slight aniseed taste. It resembles parsley in appearance. Prolonged cooking diminishes its flavour so chervil is best served fresh. There are two varieties, green and red-leafed chervil.

Chives are thin, grass-like herbs of the onion family with a hint of onion flavour. The other variety, garlic chives, have a flatter leaf with small white edible flowers and a mild garlic flavour.

Coriander, also known as cilantro or Chinese parsley, has a distinctive aroma and fresh, peppery flavour. The whole plant is used—the root, stem and leaves.

Dill is a fern-like herb, similar to fennel, with a delicate, slightly aniseed flavour and aroma. It is delicious in fish salads and vegetable salads.

Edible flowers include geraniums, nasturtiums, rose petals, marigolds, chive flowers, borage flowers and pansies. Choose unsprayed blossoms, preferably from your own garden. They are also available from supermarkets and greengrocers.

Fennel is a creamy-white, bulbous plant with feathery leaves. The bulbs can be added to salads or cooked as a vegetable and have a sweet, aniseed flavour.

Lemon grass is an aromatic herb with a sweet lemon scent. The base and tough outer layers are removed and the white interior is sliced, chopped or pounded. For salads, use the white portion just above the root.

Marjoram is a small, green herb, closely related to oregano but with a less peppery flavour.

Mint is a dark-green herb with a strong, fresh flavour. It adds a crisp, fresh taste to salads. Varieties of mint include garden, apple, Vietnamese, pineapple, spearmint and peppermint.

Mustard cress adds a peppery flavour to salads. Used as a garnish or part of a salad, it is sold in punnets at the seedling stage. Cut off the leaves as needed.

Oregano is a small-leafed herb with a strong, peppery flavour. It is often used in Greek and Italian dishes.

Parsley has a mild celery flavour and is used universally as a garnish. There are two major varieties, curly-leaf (shown) and flat-leaf parsley. Also known as Italian or continental parsley, flat-leaf parsley has a stronger flavour.

Sorrel has a large leaf and closely resembles young English spinach. It has a slightly sour taste and lemony aroma. Sorrel should not be prepared using aluminium utensils, as it will discolour.

Tarragon has a unique, tart flavour and piquant aroma. It is widely used in French cuisine and also to flavour wine vinegars and salad dressings.

Thyme is a fragrant herb with tiny pointed leaves and a pungent aroma. The most common varieties are lemon and orange thyme.

Watercress consists of small, round delicate leaves on edible stems with a peppery flavour. Buy dark leaves with no yellowing and use quickly. Trim away the coarse stems before using.

classics

CAESAR SALAD

Preparation time: 25 minutes
Total cooking time: 20 minutes
Serves 6

1 small French stick (baguette)
2 tablespoons olive oil
2 cloves garlic, halved
4 rashers bacon
2 cos lettuces
10 anchovy fillets, halved lengthways
1 cup (100 g/3½ oz) freshly shaved Parmesan
Parmesan shavings, to serve

DRESSING
2 egg yolks
4 cloves garlic, crushed
1 tablespoon Dijon mustard
4 anchovy fillets
⅓ cup (80 ml/2¾ fl oz) white wine vinegar
2 tablespoons Worcestershire sauce
1¾ cups (440 ml/14 fl oz) olive oil

1 Preheat the oven to moderate 180°C (350°F/Gas 4). Cut the bread into 15 thin slices and brush both sides with oil. Bake on a baking tray for 10–15 minutes, or until golden. Cool slightly and rub each side with the cut edge of a garlic clove. Break the bread into pieces to make croûtons.
2 Trim the bacon. Cook under a hot grill (broiler) until crisp. Drain on paper towels until cool, then break into large pieces.
3 Tear the lettuce into pieces and put in a large serving bowl with the bacon, anchovies, croûtons and Parmesan.
4 Place the egg yolks, garlic, mustard, anchovies, vinegar and Worcestershire sauce in a food processor or blender. Season and process for 20 seconds, or until smooth. With the motor running, add the oil in a thin stream until the dressing is thick and creamy. This makes enough dressing for two salads. Refrigerate the rest for up to 5 days.
5 Drizzle half the dressing over the salad and toss. Sprinkle with Parmesan.

NUTRITION PER SERVE
Protein 18 g; Fat 50 g; Carbohydrate 20 g;
Dietary Fibre 2 g; Cholesterol 55 mg; 2437 kJ
(582 Cal)

With a sharp knife, cut the anchovy fillets in half lengthways.

Rub both sides of the bread with the cut edge of the garlic clove.

Process the egg, garlic, mustard, anchovies, vinegar and Worcestershire sauce.

Add the olive oil in a thin stream until the dressing is thick and creamy.

POTATO SALAD

Preparation time: 30 minutes
Total cooking time: 5 minutes
Serves 4

600 g (1¹/₄ lb) potatoes, unpeeled,
  cut into bite-sized pieces
1 small onion, finely chopped
1 small green capsicum, chopped
2–3 celery sticks, finely chopped
¹/₄ cup (15 g/¹/₂ oz) finely chopped
  fresh parsley

DRESSING
³/₄ cup (185 g/6 oz) mayonnaise
1–2 tablespoons vinegar or lemon
  juice
2 tablespoons sour cream

1 Cook the potato in a large pan of
boiling water for 5 minutes, or until
just tender (pierce with a small sharp
knife—if the potato comes away easily
it is ready). Drain and cool completely.
2 Combine the onion, capsicum,
celery and parsley (reserving a little
for garnishing) with the cooled potato
in a large salad bowl.

3 To make the dressing, mix together
the mayonnaise, vinegar and sour
cream. Season with salt and pepper.
Pour over the salad and toss gently to
combine, without breaking the potato.
Garnish with the remaining parsley.

NUTRITION PER SERVE
Protein 6 g; Fat 20 g; Carbohydrate 30 g;
Dietary Fibre 4 g; Cholesterol 30 mg;
1355 kJ (320 Cal)

NOTE: Any potato is suitable for this
recipe. Most potatoes are delicious
with their skins left on.

Cut the potatoes into bite-sized pieces, leaving
the skins on.

Combine the onion, capsicum, celery and parsley
with the cooled potato.

Mix together the mayonnaise, vinegar and sour
cream and season, to taste.

SALAD NICOISE

Preparation time: 30 minutes
Total cooking time: 15 minutes
Serves 4

3 eggs
2 vine-ripened tomatoes
175 g (6 oz) baby green beans
1/2 cup (125 ml/4 fl oz) olive oil
2 tablespoons white wine vinegar
1 large clove garlic, halved
325 g (11 oz) iceberg lettuce heart,
    cut into 8 wedges
1 small red capsicum, seeded and
    thinly sliced
1 celery stick, cut into 5 cm (2 inch)
    thin strips
1 Lebanese cucumber, cut into thin
    5 cm (2 inch) lengths
1/4 large red onion, thinly sliced

2 x 185 g (6 oz) cans tuna, drained,
    broken into chunks
12 Kalamata olives
45 g (1 1/2 oz) can anchovy fillets,
    drained
2 teaspoons baby capers
12 small fresh basil leaves

1 Place the eggs in a saucepan of
cold water. Bring slowly to the boil,
then reduce the heat and simmer for
10 minutes. Stir during the first few
minutes to centre the yolks. Cool, then
peel and cut into quarters. Meanwhile,
score a cross in the base of each
tomato. Place in a bowl of boiling
water for 1 minute, then plunge into
cold water and peel the skin away
from the cross. Cut into eighths.
2 Trim the beans and cook them in
a saucepan of boiling water for
2 minutes, then refresh quickly under

cold water and drain. Place the oil and
vinegar in a jar and shake to combine.
3 Rub the garlic halves over the
base and sides of a large salad serving
platter. Arrange the lettuce wedges
evenly over the base. Layer the
tomato, capsicum, celery, cucumber,
beans and egg quarters over the
lettuce. Scatter with the onion and
tuna. Arrange the olives, anchovies,
capers and basil leaves over the top,
pour the dressing over the salad and
serve immediately.

NUTRITION PER SERVE
Protein 63 g; Fat 32 g; Carbohydrate 25 g;
Dietary Fibre 5 g; Cholesterol 228 mg;
2697 kJ (644 Cal)

Using a sharp knife, cut the celery stick into long, thin strips.

Cut the peeled tomatoes into quarters, and again into eighths.

Layer the tomato, capsicum, celery, cucumber, beans and egg over the lettuce.

PRAWN SALAD

Preparation time: 20 minutes
Total cooking time: Nil
Serves 6

COCKTAIL SAUCE
1 cup (250 g/8 oz) whole-egg
   mayonnaise
¼ cup (60 ml/2 fl oz) tomato sauce
2 teaspoons Worcestershire
   sauce
½ teaspoon lemon juice
1 drop Tabasco sauce

1 kg (2 lb) cooked medium prawns
lettuce, for serving
lemon wedges, for serving
sliced bread, for serving

1 For the cocktail sauce, mix all the ingredients together in a bowl, then season with salt and pepper.
2 Peel the prawns, leaving some with tails intact to use as a garnish. Remove the tails from the rest. Gently pull out the dark vein from each prawn back, starting at the head end. Add the prawns without tails to the sauce and mix to coat.
3 Arrange lettuce in serving dishes or bowls. Spoon some prawns into each dish. Garnish with the reserved prawns, drizzling with some dressing. Serve with lemon wedges and bread.

NUTRITION PER SERVE
Protein 42.5 g; Fat 16 g; Carbohydrate 34 g;
Dietary Fibre 4 g; Cholesterol 311 mg;
1900 kJ (454 Cal)

NOTE: You can make the cocktail sauce several hours ahead and refrigerate. Stir in 2 tablespoons of thick cream for a creamier sauce.

Mix all the cocktail sauce ingredients together in a bowl.

Carefully pull the shells off the prawns, leaving the tails intact.

Put the prawns in with the cocktail sauce and mix gently until well coated.

FRESH BEETROOT AND GOAT'S CHEESE SALAD

Preparation time: 20 minutes
Total cooking time: 30 minutes
Serves 4

1 kg (2 lb) (4 bulbs with leaves) fresh
    beetroot
200 g (6¹/₂ oz) green beans
1 tablespoon red wine vinegar
2 tablespoons extra virgin olive oil
1 clove garlic, crushed
1 tablespoon drained capers,
    coarsely chopped
100 g (3¹/₂ oz) goat's cheese

1 Trim the leaves from the beetroot. Scrub the bulbs and wash the leaves well. Add the whole bulbs to a large saucepan of boiling water, reduce the heat and simmer, covered, for 30 minutes, or until tender when pierced with the point of a knife. (The cooking time may vary depending on the size of the bulbs.)

2 Meanwhile, bring a saucepan of water to the boil, add the beans and cook for 3 minutes, or until just tender. Remove with a slotted spoon and plunge into a bowl of cold water. Drain well. Add the beetroot leaves to the same saucepan of boiling water and cook for 3–5 minutes, or until the leaves and stems are tender. Drain, plunge into a bowl of cold water, then drain again well.

3 Drain and cool the beetroots, then peel the skins off and cut the bulbs into thin wedges.

4 To make the dressing, put the red wine vinegar, oil, garlic, capers, ¹/₂ teaspoon salt and ¹/₂ teaspoon pepper in a screw-top jar and shake.

5 To serve, divide the beans, beetroot leaves and bulbs among four serving plates. Crumble goat's cheese over the top and drizzle with the dressing.

NUTRITION PER SERVE
Protein 12 g; Fat 18 g; Carbohydrate 22 g;
Dietary Fibre 9 g; Cholesterol 25 mg;
1256 kJ (300 Cal)

Remove the skin from the beetroot, then cut into thin wedges.

Cook the beetroot leaves until the leaves and stems are tender.

HOKKIEN NOODLE SALAD

Preparation time: 20 minutes
Total cooking time: Nil
Serves 8

900 g (1³/₄ lb) Hokkien noodles
6 spring onions, sliced diagonally
1 large red capsicum, thinly sliced
200 g (6¹/₂ oz) snow peas, sliced
1 carrot, sliced diagonally
60 g (2 oz) fresh mint, chopped
60 g (2 oz) fresh coriander, chopped
100 g (3¹/₂ oz) roasted cashew nuts

SESAME DRESSING
2 teaspoons sesame oil
1 tablespoon peanut oil
2 tablespoons lime juice
2 tablespoons kecap manis (see NOTE)
3 tablespoons sweet chilli sauce

1 Gently separate the noodles and place in a large bowl, cover with boiling water and leave for 2 minutes. Rinse and drain.
2 Put the noodles in a large bowl, and add spring onions, capsicum, snow peas, carrot, mint and coriander. Toss together well.

3 To make the dressing, whisk together the oils, lime juice, kecap manis and sweet chilli sauce. Pour the dressing over the salad and toss again. Sprinkle the cashew nuts over the top and serve immediately.

NUTRITION PER SERVE
Protein 10 g; Fat 9 g; Carbohydrate 35 g; Dietary Fibre 4.5 g; Cholesterol 0 mg; 1115 kJ (265 cal)

NOTE: If you can't find kecap manis, you can use soy sauce sweetened with a little soft brown sugar.

Top and tail the snow peas, then finely slice lengthways with a sharp knife.

Separate the noodles, then put them in a large bowl and cover with boiling water.

Whisk together the oils, lime juice, kecap manis and sweet chilli sauce.

TABBOULEH

Preparation time: 25 minutes +
  30 minutes refrigeration
Total cooking time: Nil
Serves 8

1 cup (175 g/6 oz) burghul
2 teaspoons olive oil
1 cup (30 g/1 oz) chopped fresh flat-
  leaf parsley
1 cup (50 g/1³/4 oz) chopped fresh
  mint

³/4 cup (90 g/3 oz) finely chopped
  spring onions
4 Roma (egg) tomatoes, chopped
¹/2 cup (125 ml/4 fl oz) olive oil
¹/2 cup (125 ml/4 fl oz) lemon juice
2 cloves garlic, crushed

1 Put the burghul in a bowl and pour
in 1 cup (250 ml/8 fl oz) boiling water.
Mix in the olive oil, then set aside for
10 minutes. Stir again and cool.
2 Add the herbs, spring onion and
tomato to the burghul and mix well.
Whisk the oil, lemon juice and garlic

together and add to the burghul. Mix
gently and season well. Cover and
chill for 30 minutes before serving.

NUTRITION PER SERVE
Protein 6 g; Fat 20 g; Carbohydrate 7.5 g;
Dietary Fibre 5 g; Cholesterol 0 mg;
1028 kJ (245 cal)

VARIATION: Burghul is also sold as
bulgur or cracked wheat. If you prefer,
use couscous instead of the burghul in
this recipe.

Roma tomatoes are also known as 'egg' or 'plum'
tomatoes because of their shape.

Soak the burghul in boiling water and then mix
with the olive oil.

Add the herbs, spring onion and tomato to the
burghul and mix well.

THAI BEEF SALAD WITH MINT AND CORIANDER

Preparation time: 40 minutes
Total cooking time: 4 minutes
Serves 6 as a starter

2 tablespoons dried shrimp
125 g (4 oz) English spinach
1 tablespoon sesame oil
500 g (1 lb) rump steak
1 cup (90 g/3 oz) bean sprouts
1 small red onion, thinly sliced
1 small red capsicum, cut into thin
　　strips
1 small Lebanese cucumber, cut into
　　thin strips
200 g (6$^1/_2$ oz) daikon radish, peeled
　　and cut into thin strips
1 small tomato, halved, seeded and
　　thinly sliced
$^1/_4$ cup (5 g/$^1/_4$ oz) mint leaves
$^1/_2$ cup (15 g/$^1/_2$ oz) coriander leaves
2 cloves garlic, finely chopped
1–2 small red chillies, chopped
2 small green chillies, chopped

DRESSING
$^1/_4$ cup (60 ml/2 fl oz) lime juice
$^1/_4$ cup (60 ml/2 fl oz) fish sauce
1 tablespoon finely chopped lemon
　　grass
1 teaspoon sugar

1 Soak the dried shrimp in hot water for 15 minutes; drain well and chop finely. Wash the English spinach and drain well. Trim the thick stalks and coarsely shred the leaves.
2 Heat the oil in a frying pan, add the steak and cook over high heat for 1$^1/_2$–2 minutes on each side until medium-rare. Allow to cool slightly and then slice the steak thinly.
3 To make the dressing, combine the lime juice, fish sauce, lemon grass and sugar in a small jug. Whisk until the ingredients are well combined.
4 To assemble the salad, combine the shrimp, sliced beef, bean sprouts, onion, capsicum, cucumber, radish, tomato, mint, coriander, garlic and chillies in a large bowl. Place the spinach on a serving plate, top with the combined beef and vegetables, and drizzle with the dressing.

NUTRITION PER SERVE
Protein 25 g; Fat 6 g; Carbohydrate 6 g;
Dietary Fibre 4 g; Cholesterol 65 mg;
730 kJ (175 Cal)

Slice the onion, and cut the capsicum, cucumber and daikon into thin strips.

Trim the thick stalks from the English spinach and coarsely shred the leaves.

Cook the steak over high heat for a couple of minutes until it is medium-rare.

CORONATION CHICKEN

Preparation time: 20 minutes
Total cooking time: 30 minutes
Serves 4

4 chicken breast fillets
1 carrot, chopped
1 celery stick, chopped
1/2 small onion, chopped
4 whole peppercorns
1 bay leaf
1 tablespoon oil
1 onion, chopped
2 teaspoons curry powder
1 large tomato, peeled, seeded and
    finely chopped
1/2 cup (125 ml/4 fl oz) dry white wine
2 teaspoons tomato paste
1/2 cup (125 g/4 oz) thick plain yoghurt
1/2 cup (125 g/4 oz) mayonnaise
2 teaspoons lemon juice
2 tablespoons mango chutney

1 Place the chicken, carrot, celery, onion, peppercorns and bay leaf in a single layer in a large frying pan. Add enough water to just cover the chicken. Bring to the boil, then reduce the heat and simmer for 8 minutes, or until the chicken is tender. Leave to cool in the liquid, then remove the chicken and slice into thin strips.
2 Heat the oil in a frying pan and add the onion and curry powder. Cook, stirring, for a few minutes, or until the onion is translucent. Add the chopped tomato and wine, bring to the boil, then reduce the heat and simmer for 10 minutes.
3 Stir in the tomato paste, yoghurt, mayonnaise, lemon juice and mango chutney. Mix until well combined, then season well with salt and freshly ground black pepper. Add the chicken and mix well. Serve on a bed of salad greens.

NUTRITION PER SERVE
Protein 30 g; Fat 20 g; Carbohydrate 15 g;
Dietary Fibre 3 g; Cholesterol 70 mg;
1570 kJ (375 cal)

NOTE: Coronation chicken is an English favourite and although traditionally served with a rice salad, it also makes a great sandwich filling. Use any variety of breads or crackers with some snow pea sprouts or salad greens to garnish.

Peel the tomato, remove the seeds, and finely chop the flesh.

Cover the chicken, carrot, celery, onion, peppercorns and bay leaf with water.

Stir in the tomato paste, yoghurt, mayonnaise, lemon juice and chutney.

WALDORF SALAD

Preparation time: 20 minutes
Total cooking time: Nil
Serves 4–6

2 red and 2 green apples
2 tablespoons lemon juice
¹/₄ cup (30 g/1 oz) walnut pieces
4 celery sticks, sliced
1 cup (250 g/8 oz) mayonnaise

1 Quarter the apples, remove and discard the seeds and cores, and cut the apples into small pieces.
2 Place the diced apple in a large bowl, drizzle with the lemon juice and toss to coat (this will prevent the apple discolouring). Add the walnut pieces and celery and mix well.
3 Add the mayonnaise to the apple mixture and toss until well coated. Spoon the salad into a lettuce-lined bowl and serve immediately.

NUTRITION PER SERVE (6)
Protein 2 g; Fat 15 g; Carbohydrate 20 g; Dietary Fibre 3 g; Cholesterol 15 mg; 1020 kJ (240 cal)

NOTE: Waldorf salad can be made up to 2 hours in advance and stored, covered, in the refrigerator. It is named after the Waldorf-Astoria hotel in New York where it was first served.

Using both red and green apples gives the finished salad a colourful appearance.

Pour the lemon juice over the apples and toss to coat—this will prevent them browning.

Add the mayonnaise to the apple mixture and toss until well coated.

WARM PESTO PASTA SALAD

Preparation time: 20 minutes
Total cooking time: 20 minutes
Serves 4

PESTO
2 cloves garlic, crushed
1 teaspoon sea salt
3 tablespoons pine nuts, toasted
2 cups (60 g/2 oz) fresh basil
1/2 cup (50 g/1³/4 oz) grated
    Parmesan
1/3 cup (80 ml/2³/4 fl oz) extra virgin
    olive oil

500 g (1 lb) orecchiette or shell pasta
2 tablespoons olive oil
150 g (5 oz) jar capers, drained and
    patted dry
2 tablespoons extra virgin olive oil
2 cloves garlic, chopped
3 tomatoes, seeded and diced
300 g (10 oz) thin asparagus spears,
    cut in half and blanched
2 tablespoons balsamic vinegar
200 g (6¹/2 oz) rocket, trimmed and
    cut into short lengths
Parmesan shavings, to garnish

1 To make the pesto, place the garlic, sea salt and pine nuts in a food processor or blender and process until combined. Add the basil and Parmesan and process until finely minced. With the motor running, add the oil in a thin steady stream and blend until smooth.
2 Cook the pasta in a large saucepan of boiling water until *al dente*, then drain well.
3 Meanwhile, heat the oil in a frying pan, add the capers and fry over high heat, stirring occasionally, for 4–5 minutes, or until crisp. Remove from the pan and drain on crumpled paper towels.
4 In the same frying pan, heat the extra virgin olive oil over medium heat and add the garlic, tomato and asparagus. Cook for 1–2 minutes, or until warmed through, tossing well. Stir in the balsamic vinegar.
5 Drain the pasta and transfer to a large serving bowl. Add the pesto and toss, coating the pasta well. Cool slightly. Add the tomato mixture and rocket and season to taste with salt and cracked black pepper. Toss well and sprinkle with the capers and Parmesan. Serve warm.

NUTRITION PER SERVE
Protein 22 g; Fat 45 g; Carbohydrate 90 g;
Dietary Fibre 9 g; Cholesterol 12 mg;
3629 kJ (868 cal)

Fry the capers over high heat, stirring occasionally, until crisp.

Add the pesto and toss thoroughly through the pasta. Allow to cool a little.

25

GREEK SALAD

Preparation time: 20 minutes
Total cooking time: Nil
Serves 6–8

6 tomatoes, cut into thin wedges
1 red onion, cut into thin rings
2 Lebanese cucumbers, sliced
1 cup (185 g/6 oz) Kalamata olives
200 g (6¹/2 oz) feta cheese
¹/2 cup (125 ml/4 fl oz) extra virgin olive oil
dried oregano, to sprinkle

1 Combine the tomato wedges with the onion rings, sliced cucumber and Kalamata olives in a large bowl. Season to taste with salt and freshly ground black pepper.

2 Break up the feta into large pieces with your fingers and scatter over the top of the salad. Drizzle with the olive oil and sprinkle with some oregano.

NUTRITION PER SERVE (8)
Protein 6 g; Fat 25 g; Carbohydrate 3 g;
Dietary Fibre 2 g; Cholesterol 15 mg;
1060 kJ (250 cal)

Cut the tomatoes into thin wedges, and cut the red onion into thin rings.

Combine the tomato, onion, cucumber and olives in a large bowl.

Good feta should break up and crumble nicely. Just use your fingers.

CARAMELIZED ONION AND POTATO SALAD

Preparation time: 20 minutes
Total cooking time: 1 hour

oil, for cooking
6 red onions, thinly sliced
1 kg (2 lb) small waxy potatoes, unpeeled
4 rashers bacon, rind removed
2/3 cup (30 g/1 oz) fresh chives, snipped
1 cup (250 g/8 oz) mayonnaise
1 tablespoon Dijon mustard
juice of 1 lemon
2 tablespoons sour cream

1 Heat 2 tablespoons of oil in a large heavy-based frying pan, add the onion and cook over medium-low heat for 40 minutes, or until very soft.
2 Cut the potatoes into large chunks (if they are small enough, leave them whole). Cook in boiling water for 10 minutes, or until just tender, then drain and cool slightly. (Do not overcook the potatoes or they will fall apart.)
3 Grill (broil) the bacon until crisp, drain on paper towels and cool slightly before coarsely chopping.
4 Put the potato, onion and chives in a large bowl, reserving a few chives for a garnish, and mix well.
5 Put the mayonnaise, mustard, lemon juice and sour cream in a bowl and whisk together. Pour over the salad and toss to coat. Sprinkle with the bacon and garnish with the reserved chives.

NUTRITION PER SERVE
Protein 9 g; Fat 13 g; Carbohydrate 35 g; Dietary Fibre 4.5 g; Cholesterol 20 mg; 1221 kJ (292 Cal)

Cook the sliced onion over medium-low heat until soft and caramelized.

Wash the potatoes and cut them into large chunks or leave whole if they are small enough.

Whisk together the mayonnaise, mustard, lemon juice and sour cream.

GADO GADO

Preparation time: 30 minutes
Total cooking time: 35 minutes
Serves 4

6 new potatoes, unpeeled
2 carrots, cut into thick strips
250 g (8 oz) snake beans, cut into
    10 cm (4 inch) lengths
2 tablespoons peanut oil
250 g (8 oz) firm tofu, cubed
100 g (3^1/$_2$ oz) baby English spinach
2 Lebanese cucumbers, cut into thick
    strips
1 large red capsicum, thickly sliced
100 g (3^1/$_2$ oz) bean sprouts
5 hard-boiled eggs

PEANUT SAUCE
1 tablespoon peanut oil
1 onion, finely chopped
^{2}/$_3$ cup (160 g/5^1/$_2$ oz) peanut butter
^{1}/$_4$ cup (60 ml/2 fl oz) kecap manis
2 tablespoons ground coriander
2 teaspoons chilli sauce
^{3}/$_4$ cup (185 ml/6 fl oz) coconut cream
1 teaspoon grated palm sugar
1 tablespoon lemon juice

1 Cook the potatoes in boiling water until tender. Drain and cool slightly. Cut into quarters. Cook the carrots and beans separately in pans of boiling water until just tender. Plunge into iced water, then drain.
2 Heat the oil in a non-stick frying pan and cook the tofu in batches until crisp. Drain on paper towels.
3 To make the peanut sauce, heat the oil in a pan over low heat and cook the onion for 5 minutes, or until golden. Add the peanut butter, kecap manis, coriander, chilli sauce and coconut cream. Bring to the boil, reduce the heat and simmer for 5 minutes. Add the sugar and juice and stir until dissolved.
4 Arrange the vegetables and tofu on a plate. Halve the eggs and place in the centre. Serve with the sauce.

NUTRITION PER SERVE
Protein 35 g; Fat 55 g; Carbohydrate 35 g;
Dietary Fibre 15 g; Cholesterol 265 mg;
3175 kJ (755 cal)

Cut the cucumbers and capsicum into thick strips for dipping in the sauce.

Cook the snake beans quickly in a large saucepan of boiling water.

Heat the oil and cook the tofu in batches until crisp and golden brown.

Add the peanut butter, kecap manis, coriander, chilli sauce and coconut cream.

CURLY ENDIVE SALAD WITH CRISP PROSCIUTTO AND GARLIC CROUTONS

Preparation time: 20 minutes
Total cooking time: 5 minutes
Serves 6

1 large bunch curly endive
1/2 red oak leaf lettuce
2 red onions
4 slices white or brown bread
2 large cloves garlic, crushed
60 g (2 oz) butter, softened
30 g (1 oz) feta cheese, mashed
4–6 thin slices prosciutto
1 large avocado

DRESSING
2 tablespoons olive oil
3 tablespoons sugar
3 tablespoons spicy tomato sauce
1 tablespoon soy sauce
1/3 cup (80 ml/2³/4 fl oz) red wine
    vinegar

1 Tear the endive and lettuce into pieces. Peel and slice the onions and separate into rings. Toss the endive, lettuce and onion in a salad bowl.
2 Toast the bread on one side only. Mash the garlic, butter and feta cheese into a paste and spread over the untoasted side of the bread. Remove the crusts and toast the buttered side of the bread until crisp and golden. Cut into small cubes.
3 Crisp the prosciutto under a very hot grill (broiler) for a few seconds. Remove and cut into pieces. Cut the avocado into thin wedges.
4 To make the dressing, whisk the oil, sugar, tomato sauce, soy sauce and vinegar together. Add the prosciutto and avocado to the salad and pour over half the dressing. Arrange the croutons on top and serve the remaining dressing in a jug.

NUTRITION PER SERVE
Protein 5 g; Fat 24 g; Carbohydrate 22 g; Dietary Fibre 2 g; Cholesterol 27 mg; 1356 kJ (324 Cal)

STORAGE: The dressing will keep for a day in a screw-top jar.

Peel the red onion, slice it thinly and then separate into rings.

Spread the feta, butter and garlic paste over the untoasted side of the bread.

Crisp the prosciutto under a hot grill and then cut it into pieces.

Whisk together the oil, sugar, tomato sauce, soy sauce and vinegar.

CHARGRILLED BABY OCTOPUS SALAD

Preparation time: 30 minutes +
  2 hours refrigeration
Total cooking time: 15 minutes
Serves 4 as an entrée

1 kg (2 lb) baby octopus
1 teaspoon sesame oil
2 tablespoons lime juice
2 tablespoons fish sauce
1/4 cup (60 ml/2 fl oz) sweet chilli
  sauce
200 g (6 1/2 oz) mixed salad leaves
1 red capsicum, very thinly sliced
2 small Lebanese cucumbers, seeded
  and cut into ribbons
4 red Asian shallots, chopped
100 g (3 1/2 oz) toasted unsalted
  peanuts, chopped

1 To clean the octopus, remove the head from the tentacles by cutting just underneath the eyes. To clean the head, carefully slit the head open and remove the gut. Cut it in half. Push out the beak from the centre of the tentacles, then cut the tentacles into sets of four or two, depending on their size. Pull the skin away from the head and tentacles if it comes away easily. The eyes will come off as you pull off the skin.

2 To make the marinade, combine the sesame oil, lime juice, fish sauce and sweet chilli sauce in a shallow non-metallic bowl. Add the octopus, and stir to coat. Cover and refrigerate for 2 hours.

3 Heat a chargrill pan or barbecue to very hot. Drain the octopus, reserving the marinade, then cook in batches for 3–5 minutes, turning occasionally.

4 Pour the marinade into a saucepan, bring to the boil and cook for 2 minutes, or until it has thickened.

5 Divide the salad leaves among four plates, scatter with capsicum and cucumber, then top with the octopus. Drizzle with the marinade and sprinkle with the red Asian shallots and peanuts.

NUTRITION PER SERVE
Protein 50 g; Fat 17 g; Carbohydrate 9 g;
Dietary Fibre 5 g; Cholesterol 500 mg;
1622 kJ (387 Cal)

Remove the head from the tentacles by cutting just underneath the eyes.

To clean the head, slit the head open and remove the gut.

Push the beak out from the centre of the tentacles.

Pull the skin away from the head and tentacles if it comes away easily.

TOMATO, AVOCADO AND BACON PASTA SALAD

Preparation time: 15 minutes
Total cooking time: 25 minutes
Serves 4

4 cloves garlic, unpeeled
1/3 cup (80 ml/2³/4 fl oz) olive oil
250 g (8 oz) cherry tomatoes
300 g (10 oz) short cut bacon
    (see NOTE)
350 g (11 oz) fresh fettucine
1 tablespoon white wine vinegar
2 tablespoons roughly chopped
    fresh basil
2 ripe avocados, diced
whole fresh basil leaves,
    to garnish

1 Preheat the oven to moderately hot 200°C (400°F/Gas 6). Place the garlic at one end of a roasting tin and drizzle with 2 tablespoons of the olive oil. Place the tomatoes at the other end and season well. Bake for 10 minutes, then remove the garlic. Return the tomatoes to the oven for a further 5–10 minutes, or until soft.
2 Cook the bacon under a hot grill (broiler) for 4–5 minutes each side, or until crisp and golden. Roughly chop. Meanwhile, cook the pasta in a large saucepan of boiling water until *al dente*. Drain well and transfer to a large bowl. Drizzle 1 tablespoon of the olive oil over the pasta and toss well. Season to taste with salt and freshly ground black pepper and keep warm.

3 Slit the skin of each garlic clove and squeeze the garlic out. Place in a screw-top jar with the vinegar, chopped basil and remaining oil and shake well to combine. Add the tomatoes and their juices, bacon and avocado to the fettucine, pour on the dressing and toss well. Garnish with the basil leaves and serve with a green salad and crusty bread.

NUTRITION PER SERVE
Protein 27.5 g; Fat 44 g; Carbohydrate 50.5 g;
Dietary Fibre 4 g; Cholesterol 106.5 mg;
2960 kJ (705 Cal)

NOTE: Short cut bacon is the meaty end of the bacon rasher and is also sold as eye bacon.

Bake the tomatoes until they are wrinkled and quite soft.

Grill the bacon until it is crisp and golden, but take care to not burn it.

The roasted garlic should slip out of its skin quite easily.

31

LEBANESE TOASTED BREAD SALAD (FATTOUSH)

Preparation time: 15 minutes
Total cooking time: 10 minutes
Serves 6

2 pitta bread rounds (17 cm/7 inches diameter)
6 cos lettuce leaves, shredded
1 large Lebanese cucumber, cubed
4 tomatoes, cut into 1 cm (1/2 inch) cubes
8 spring onions, chopped
4 tablespoons finely chopped fresh flat-leaf parsley

1 tablespoon finely chopped fresh mint
2 tablespoons finely chopped fresh coriander

DRESSING
2 cloves garlic, crushed
100 ml (3 1/2 fl oz) extra virgin olive oil
100 ml (3 1/2 fl oz) lemon juice

1 Preheat the oven to moderate 180°C (350°F/Gas 4). Split the bread in half through the centre and bake on a baking tray for 8–10 minutes, or until golden and crisp, turning halfway through. Break into pieces.
2 To make the dressing, whisk all the ingredients together in a bowl.

3 Place the bread and remaining salad ingredients in a serving bowl and toss to combine. Pour on the dressing and toss well. Season to taste with salt and freshly ground black pepper. Serve immediately.

NUTRITION PER SERVE
Protein 5.5 g; Fat 17 g; Carbohydrate 24 g;
Dietary Fibre 4 g; Cholesterol 0 mg;
1133 kJ (270 Cal)

NOTE: This is a popular Middle Eastern peasant salad which is served as an appetiser or to accompany a light meal.

Split the pitta bread rounds in two through the centre.

Once the bread is golden and crisp, break it into small pieces with your fingers.

Place the bread pieces and salad ingredients in a bowl and toss well.

VIETNAMESE CHICKEN AND CABBAGE SALAD

Preparation time: 40 minutes
Total cooking time: 5 minutes
Serves 4

4 cooked chicken thigh fillets
1 cup (125 g/4 oz) thinly sliced
  celery
2 carrots, cut into thin strips
1 cup (75 g/2¹/₂ oz) finely shredded
  cabbage
1 small onion, sliced
¹/₄ cup (7 g/¹/₄ oz) fresh coriander
  leaves
¹/₄ cup (15 g/¹/₂ oz) finely shredded
  fresh mint

DRESSING
¹/₄ cup (60 g/2 oz) caster sugar
1 tablespoon fish sauce
1 teaspoon crushed garlic
2 tablespoons white vinegar
1 red chilli, seeded and finely chopped

TOPPING
2 tablespoons peanut oil
1¹/₂ teaspoons chopped garlic
¹/₃ cup (50 g/1³/₄ oz) roasted peanuts,
  finely chopped
1 tablespoon caster sugar

1 Cut the chicken fillets into long, thin strips. Combine the chicken, celery, carrot, cabbage, onion, coriander and mint in a large bowl.
2 To make the dressing, put the sugar, fish sauce, garlic, vinegar, chilli and 2 tablespoons water in a small bowl. Whisk until the sugar has dissolved and the ingredients are well combined. Pour the dressing over the chicken mixture and toss to combine. Arrange on a serving plate.
3 To make the topping, heat the oil in a wok over moderate heat. Add the garlic and cook, stirring, until pale golden. Stir in the peanuts and sugar. Cool slightly. Sprinkle the topping over the salad just before serving.

NUTRITION PER SERVE
Protein 50 g; Fat 15 g; Carbohydrate 25 g;
Dietary Fibre 3 g; Cholesterol 110 mg;
1820 kJ (435 cal)

Combine the chicken, celery, carrot, cabbage, onion, coriander and mint.

Pour the dressing over the salad and gently toss to combine.

Gently stir the peanuts and sugar into the cooked garlic.

RICE SALAD

Preparation time: 30 minutes
  + 1 hour refrigeration
Total cooking time: 20 minutes
Serves 6–8

1¹/₂ cups (300 g/10 oz) long-grain rice
¹/₂ cup (80 g/2³/₄ oz) fresh or frozen
    peas
3 spring onions, sliced
1 green capsicum, finely diced
1 red capsicum, finely diced
310 g (10 oz) can corn kernels
¹/₄ cup (15 g/¹/₂ oz) chopped mint

DRESSING
¹/₂ cup (125 ml/4 fl oz) extra virgin
    olive oil
2 tablespoons lemon juice
1 clove garlic, crushed
1 teaspoon sugar

1 Bring a large pan of water to the boil and stir in the rice. Return to the boil and cook for 12–15 minutes, or until tender. Drain and cool.
2 Cook the peas in a small pan of boiling water for about 2 minutes. Rinse under cold water and drain well.
3 To make the dressing, combine the oil, lemon juice, garlic and sugar in a small jug and whisk until well blended. Season with salt and pepper.
4 Combine the rice, peas, spring onion, capsicum, corn and mint in a large bowl. Add the dressing and mix well. Cover and refrigerate for 1 hour. Transfer to a serving dish to serve.

NUTRITION PER SERVE (8)
Protein 5 g; Fat 15 g; Carbohydrate 40 g;
Dietary Fibre 3 g; Cholesterol 0 mg;
1350 kJ (320 cal)

Slice the spring onions and finely dice the capsicums, removing the white membrane.

Cook the peas in a pan of boiling water for 2 minutes.

Combine the rice, vegetables and mint and drizzle with the dressing.

HOT POTATO SALAD

Preparation time: 15 minutes
Total cooking time: 30 minutes
Serves 6–8

4 rashers bacon (optional)
1½ kg (3 lb) small Desiree potatoes
4 spring onions, sliced
¼ cup (7 g/¼ oz) chopped flat-leaf
　　parsley
½ teaspoon salt

DRESSING
⅔ cup (170 ml/5½ fl oz) extra virgin
　　olive oil
1 tablespoon Dijon mustard
⅓ cup (80 ml) white wine vinegar

1 Trim the rind and excess fat from the bacon. Cook under a hot grill (broiler) until crisp. Chop into small pieces.
2 Bring a large heavy-based pan of water to the boil. Add the potatoes and simmer until just tender, trying not to let the skins break away too much. Drain and cool slightly.
3 To make the dressing, whisk the ingredients in a jug until well blended.
4 Cut the potatoes into quarters and place in a large bowl with half the bacon, the spring onion, parsley, salt and some freshly ground black pepper. Pour in half the dressing and toss gently to coat the potatoes.
5 Transfer to a serving bowl, drizzle with the remaining dressing and sprinkle with the remaining bacon.

NUTRITION PER SERVE (8)
Protein 8 g; Fat 20 g; Carbohydrate 25 g;
Dietary Fibre 3 g; Cholesterol 10 mg;
1365 kJ (325 Cal)

Using a small, sharp knife, trim the rind and excess fat from the bacon.

Whisk the dressing ingredients in a small jug until well blended.

When the potatoes are just cool enough to handle, cut them into quarters.

SPINACH SALAD

Preparation time: 20 minutes
Total cooking time: 20 minutes
Serves 2–4

3 slices white bread, crusts removed
150 g (5 oz) English spinach leaves
2–3 tablespoons pine nuts
3 rashers bacon, chopped
8 button mushrooms, finely sliced
1/4 cup (7 g/1/4 oz) basil leaves,
   shredded
1–2 cloves garlic, crushed
2–3 tablespoons olive oil

balsamic vinegar or freshly squeezed
   lemon juice, to taste

1 Preheat the oven to moderately hot 190°C (375°F/Gas 5). Cut the bread into small cubes, spread on a baking tray and bake for 10 minutes, or until the bread cubes are golden.
2 Gently rinse the spinach leaves under cold water. Bundle them in a clean tea towel and shake gently to remove the water. Tear into pieces and place in a large serving bowl. Put the pine nuts in a non-stick frying pan and stir gently over low heat until golden brown. Remove and cool slightly. Add

the bacon to the pan and cook for 5–6 minutes, or until crispy. Remove and drain on paper towels.
3 Add the pine nuts, bacon, bread cubes, mushrooms and basil to the spinach leaves. Whisk the garlic and oil together and pour over the salad, mixing gently. Drizzle with the vinegar or lemon juice. Sprinkle with salt and freshly ground pepper, and serve immediately.

NUTRITION PER SERVE (4)
Protein 10 g; Fat 20 g; Carbohydrate 10 g;
Dietary Fibre 3 g; Cholesterol 15 mg;
1105 kJ (265 Cal)

Cut the bread into small cubes and spread on a baking tray.

Bundle the spinach leaves in a tea towel and shake to remove the excess water.

Pour the combined garlic and oil over the salad, mixing gently.

BEAN SALAD

Preparation time: 30 minutes
Total cooking time: 5 minutes
Serves 8–10

250 g (8 oz) green beans, topped
   and tailed
400 g (13 oz) can chickpeas, drained
   and rinsed
425 g (14 oz) can red kidney beans,
   drained and rinsed
400 g (13 oz) can cannellini beans,
   drained and rinsed
270 g (9 oz) can corn kernels, drained
   and rinsed
3 spring onions, sliced
1 red capsicum, finely chopped
3 celery sticks, chopped
4–6 gherkins, chopped (optional)
1/4 cup (15 g/1/2 oz) chopped mint
1/4 cup (7 g/1/4 oz) chopped flat-leaf
   parsley

MUSTARD VINAIGRETTE
1 quantity Basic Vinaigrette
1 tablespoon Dijon mustard
1 clove garlic, crushed

1 Cut the green beans into short
lengths. Bring a small pan of water to
the boil, add the beans and cook for
2 minutes. Drain and rinse under cold
water then leave in a bowl of iced
water until cold. Drain well.
2 Place the beans, chickpeas, kidney
beans, cannellini beans, corn, spring
onion, capsicum, celery, gherkin, mint
and parsley in a large bowl. Season
with salt and freshly ground black
pepper and mix until well combined.
3 To make the Mustard Vinaigrette,
whisk together the Basic Vinaigrette,
mustard and crushed garlic until
combined. Drizzle over the salad and
toss gently to combine. Transfer to a
large serving bowl or platter.

NUTRITION PER SERVE (10)
Protein 10 g; Fat 15 g; Carbohydrate 25 g;
Dietary Fibre 10 g; Cholesterol 0 mg;
1090 kJ (260 Cal)

NOTE: Prepare the salad up to 3 hours
in advance, cover and refrigerate. Add
the dressing just before serving.

Cut the vegetables into small dice, trying to make
them all a similar size.

Add the beans to a pan of boiling water and cook
for 2 minutes.

starters & sides

SMOKED SALMON SALAD WITH POTATO ROSTI AND HORSERADISH CREAM

Preparation time: 45 minutes
Total cooking time: 30 minutes
Serves 4 as an entrée

1 cup (30 g/1 oz) watercress sprigs
1 green coral or other loose-leafed
    lettuce, shredded
100 g (3¹/2 oz) baby rocket, trimmed
2 heads of witlof, sliced into
    1.5 cm (5/8 inch) pieces
400 g (13 oz) smoked salmon

HORSERADISH CREAM
¹/3 cup (80 ml/2³/4 fl oz) cream
¹/2 red onion, chopped
1 tablespoon lemon juice
1¹/2 tablespoons horseradish

RÖSTI
1 egg
2 tablespoons plain flour
550 g (1 lb 4 oz) russet or other
    starchy potatoes, grated
¹/2 cup (80 g/2³/4 oz) grated onion
2 teaspoons oil
40 g (1¹/2 oz) butter

1 Toss all the greens together in a large bowl and set aside.
2 To make the horseradish cream, place the cream, red onion, lemon juice, ¹/4 teaspoon salt and ¹/4 teaspoon cracked black pepper in a small saucepan and simmer for 2 minutes, or until thickened slightly. Add the horseradish and remove from the heat.
3 To make the rösti, preheat the oven to moderately hot 190°C (375°/Gas 5). Whisk the egg and flour together in a

bowl. Squeeze any excess moisture out of the potatoes. Stir the potato into the egg mixture, then add the onion and ¹/4 teaspoon each salt and pepper.
4 Heat the oil and butter in a large frying pan over medium heat. Form the potato into four even-sized balls. Add the balls in batches and press down with an egg flip to form 10 cm (4 inch) patties. Cook for 4–5 minutes each side, or until deep brown. Transfer to the oven and cook for 5–7 minutes, or until the outside is crusty and the inside is soft.

5 Just before serving, warm the horseradish cream. Arrange a quarter of the smoked salmon on each plate, with the tips of the salmon slices overlapping in the middle. Place a rösti over the salmon and top with a quarter of the greens. Drizzle with horseradish cream and serve.

NUTRITION PER SERVE
Protein 30 g; Fat 26 g; Carbohydrate 28 g; Dietary Fibre 5 g; Cholesterol 147 mg; 1965 kJ (469 Cal)

Simmer the horseradish cream until slightly thickened.

Squeeze the excess moisture out of the grated potato.

Using an egg flip, press the balls of potato into 10 cm patties.

LEMON, FENNEL AND ROCKET SALAD

Preparation time: 25 minutes
Total cooking time: 5 minutes
Serves 4

2 lemons
2 oranges
1 large fennel bulb or 2 baby fennel
200 g (6¹/₂ oz) rocket
100 g (3¹/₂ oz) pecans, chopped
¹/₂ cup (90 g/3 oz) stuffed green
    olives, halved lengthways

TOASTED SESAME DRESSING
1 tablespoon sesame oil
1 tablespoon sesame seeds
¹/₄ cup (60 ml/2 fl oz) olive oil
2 tablespoons white wine vinegar
1 teaspoon French mustard

1 Peel the lemons and oranges, removing all the white pith. Cut the fruit into thin slices and remove any seeds. Thinly slice the fennel. Wash and dry the rocket leaves and tear into pieces. Chill the salad while making the dressing.
2 To make the dressing, heat the oil in a small pan over moderate heat. Add the sesame seeds and fry, stirring constantly, until lightly golden. Remove from the heat and cool. Pour the mixture into a small jug, whisk in the remaining ingredients and season with salt and ground black pepper.
3 Combine the fruit, fennel, rocket, pecans and olives in a shallow serving bowl. Drizzle with the dressing.

NUTRITION PER SERVE
Protein 6 g; Fat 40 g; Carbohydrate 10 g;
Dietary Fibre 9 g; Cholesterol 0 mg;
1820 kJ (435 Cal)

Cut the peeled lemons and oranges into thin slices and remove any seeds.

Using a large, sharp knife, thinly slice the fennel bulb crossways.

Stir the sesame seeds in the sesame oil until they are lightly golden.

41

MARINATED GRILLED VEGETABLE SALAD

Preparation time: 30 minutes + 1 hour
  marinating
Total cooking time: 5 minutes
Serves 6

3 small slender eggplants
2 small red capsicums
3 zucchini
6 mushrooms

MARINADE
3 tablespoons olive oil
3 tablespoons lemon juice
3 tablespoons shredded basil leaves
1 clove garlic, crushed

1 Cut the eggplant into diagonal slices. Place on a tray in a single layer, sprinkle with salt and leave for 15 minutes. Rinse thoroughly and pat dry with paper towels. Trim the capsicum, remove the seeds and membrane and cut into long, wide pieces. Cut the zucchini into diagonal slices. Trim each mushroom stalk so that it is level with the cap. Place all the vegetables in a large, shallow non-metallic dish.

2 To make the marinade, put the oil, juice, basil and garlic in a small screw-top jar. Shake vigorously to combine. Pour over the vegetables and toss well. Store, covered with plastic wrap, in the fridge for 1 hour, stirring occasionally.
3 Cook the vegetables on a hot, lightly oiled barbecue grill or flatplate. Cook each vegetable piece over the hottest part of the fire for 2 minutes on each side, brushing frequently with any remaining marinade.

NUTRITION PER SERVE
Protein 1 g; Fat 10 g; Carbohydrate 2 g; Dietary Fibre 2 g; Cholesterol 0 mg; 445 kJ (110 Cal)

STORAGE: The vegetables can be marinated for up to 2 hours before cooking. Take the vegetables out of the fridge 15 minutes before cooking to allow the oil in the marinade to soften. Once cooked, they can be served warm or cold. The marinade can also be used as a salad dressing. Make up extra and store in the fridge, in a screw-top jar, for up to 2 weeks.

Put the vegetables in a shallow, non-metallic dish and pour over the marinade.

Cook the vegetables over the hottest part of the fire for 2 minutes on each side.

DEEP-FRIED CALAMARI AND PARSLEY SALAD

Preparation time: 15 minutes +
  30 minutes standing
Total cooking time: 10 minutes
Serves 4 as an entrée

DEEP-FRIED CALAMARI
150 g (5 oz) besan (chickpea flour)
1½ teaspoons bittersweet smoked
  paprika or normal paprika
1½ teaspoons ground cumin
½ teaspoon baking powder
1 cup (250 ml/8 fl oz) soda water
oil, for deep-frying
6 calamari, cleaned and sliced
  into rings 8 mm (¼ inch) wide

PARSLEY SALAD
¼ preserved lemon, rinsed, pith
  and flesh removed
¼ cup (60 ml/2 fl oz) lemon juice
¼ cup (60 ml/2 fl oz) extra virgin olive
  oil
1 clove garlic, finely chopped
1 cup (20 g/¾ oz) flat-leaf parsley
harissa, to serve (optional)

1 To make the batter, sift the besan, paprika, cumin and baking powder into a bowl, add ¼ teaspoon pepper, mix together and make a well in the centre. Gradually add the soda water, whisking until smooth. Season with salt. Cover, then leave for 30 minutes.
2 Cut the lemon rind into very thin slivers. To make the dressing, whisk the lemon juice, extra virgin olive oil and garlic together in a bowl.
3 Fill a large heavy-based saucepan or wok one third full of oil and heat until a cube of bread dropped into the oil browns in 15 seconds.
4 Dip the calamari into the batter, allowing any excess to drip away.

Cook in batches for 30–60 seconds, or until pale gold and crisp all over. Drain well on crumpled paper towels and keep warm.
5 Add the parsley and lemon slivers to the dressing, tossing to coat the leaves. Divide the leaves among four bowls or plates. Top with the calamari rings and serve with harissa.

NUTRITION PER SERVE
Protein 14 g; Fat 27 g; Carbohydrate 14 g;
Dietary Fibre 5 g; Cholesterol 90 mg;
1470 kJ (350 Cal)

Whisk the batter ingredients together until smooth.

Using a sharp knife, cut the lemon rind into very thin slivers.

STUFFED MUSHROOM SALAD

Preparation time: 25 minutes
Total cooking time: Nil
Serves 4

20 button mushrooms
1/4 cup (60 g/2 oz) pesto, chilled
100 g (3 1/2 oz) rocket leaves
1 green oakleaf lettuce
12 small black olives
1/3 cup (50 g/1 3/4 oz) sliced semi-dried
   or sun-dried tomatoes
1 tablespoon roughly chopped
   basil
Parmesan shavings, to serve

DRESSING
1/3 cup (80 ml/2 3/4 fl oz) olive oil
1 tablespoon white wine vinegar
1 teaspoon Dijon mustard

1 Trim the mushroom stalks level with the caps and scoop out the remaining stalk with a melon baller. Spoon the pesto into the mushrooms.
2 To make the dressing, whisk together all the ingredients. Season with salt and pepper, to taste.
3 Arrange the rocket and lettuce leaves on a serving plate and top with the mushrooms, olives, tomato and basil. Drizzle the dressing over the salad and top with the Parmesan shavings. Serve immediately.

NUTRITION PER SERVE
Protein 9 g; Fat 35 g; Carbohydrate 2 g;
Dietary Fibre 3 g; Cholesterol 15 mg;
1525 kJ (365 cal)

HINT: Home-made pesto is preferable for this recipe. To make your own, process 1 cup (30 g/1 oz) loosely packed basil leaves, 2 tablespoons pine nuts and 1/4 cup (25 g/3/4 oz) grated Parmesan in a food processor to form a smooth paste. Gradually pour in 1/4 cup (60 ml/2 fl oz) olive oil in a steady stream with the motor running. Process until combined.

Draw a vegetable peeler across a block of Parmesan to make the shavings.

Trim the mushroom stalks so they are level with the caps.

Spoon the chilled pesto into the mushroom caps. Home-made pesto will give the best flavour.

CRAB, MANGO AND PASTA SALAD

Preparation time: 15 minutes
Total cooking time: 12 minutes
Serves 4

150 g (5 oz) rocket
125 g (4 oz) dried saffron fettucine
125 g (4 oz) dried squid ink
    fettucine
1 mango, cut into thin strips
1 avocado, sliced
1 red onion, cut into thin wedges
500 g (1 lb) fresh or frozen crab
    meat

DRESSING
1/4 cup (60 ml/2 fl oz) olive oil
1 tablespoon whole-egg mayonnaise
2 tablespoons lime juice
1 clove garlic, crushed
1/4 teaspoon lime oil or grated lime
    zest

1 Trim any long stems from the rocket, rinse and dry. Cook the fettucine in a saucepan of rapidly boiling salted water for 12 minutes, or until al dente. Drain, cool, then return to the saucepan.
2 For the dressing, combine all the ingredients together in a bowl and whisk thoroughly. Toss through the cooled fettucine.
3 Arrange nests of the fettucine on each serving plate, then top each with some rocket, mango, avocado, red onion and crab meat. Season with salt and freshly ground black pepper, to taste. Delicious served with slices of crusty bread.

NUTRITION PER SERVE
Protein 24.5 g; Fat 26.5 g; Carbohydrate 50 g; Dietary Fibre 5.5 g; Cholesterol 107 mg; 2255 kJ (540 Cal)

With a sharp knife, cut the mango flesh into thin strips.

Pull off any long stems from the rocket, then rinse the leaves and pat dry.

When the fettucine has cooled, toss the dressing through until well coated.

MUSSEL SALAD WITH SAFFRON DRESSING

Preparation time: 40 minutes
Total cooking time: 30 minutes
Serves 4–6

750 g (1 1/2 lb) baby new potatoes,
    unpeeled
1.5 kg (3 lb) black mussels
2/3 cup (170 ml/5 1/2 fl oz) dry white
    wine
1 small onion, sliced
2 sprigs thyme
2 bay leaves
large pinch saffron threads
1/2 cup (125 g/4 oz) sour cream
1 tablespoon finely chopped flat-leaf
    parsley

1 Place the potatoes in a saucepan of lightly salted water. Bring to the boil, then reduce the heat and simmer for 20 minutes, or until tender. (When pierced with the point of a knife, the potato will come away.) Drain and leave to cool. If using large potatoes, cut into quarters or halves.
2 Scrub the mussels with a stiff brush and pull out the hairy beards. Discard any broken mussels, or open ones that don't close when tapped on the bench. Rinse thoroughly. Place the wine, onion, thyme sprigs, bay leaves and half the mussels in a saucepan with a tight-fitting lid. Cover and cook over high heat, stirring once, for about 4–5 minutes, or until the mussels start to open. Remove the mussels as they open, using tongs. Discard any unopened mussels. Cook the remaining mussels the same way, and leave to cool.
3 Strain the mussel cooking liquid and reserve 1/3 cup (80 ml/2 3/4 fl oz). While still warm, stir in the saffron. Cool, then gradually whisk the mussel liquid into the sour cream and season well with salt and cracked pepper. Stir in the chopped parsley.
4 Remove the flesh from the mussels and discard the shells. Put the mussels and potatoes in a bowl, add the dressing and toss gently to coat.

NUTRITION PER SERVE (6)
Protein 18.5 g; Fat 11.3 g; Carbohydrate 23 g; Dietary Fibre 2.5 g; Cholesterol 62.5 mg; 1235 kJ (292 Cal)

Gradually whisk the mussel liquid into the sour cream until smooth.

Gently toss the saffron dressing through the mussels and potatoes.

ASPARAGUS AND RED CAPSICUM SALAD

Preparation time: 20 minutes
Total cooking time: 15 minutes
Serves 4

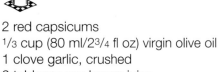

2 red capsicums
1/3 cup (80 ml/2¾ fl oz) virgin olive oil
1 clove garlic, crushed
2 tablespoons lemon juice
2 tablespoons chopped basil
2 tablespoons pine nuts
310 g (10 oz) fresh asparagus
small black olives

1 Cut the capsicums into large pieces, removing the seeds and white membrane. Place, skin-side-up, under a hot grill (broiler) until the skin blackens and blisters. Cool under a tea towel or in a plastic bag, then carefully peel away and discard the skin. Finely dice the capsicum flesh.
2 Put the olive oil, garlic, lemon juice and basil in a small bowl and whisk to combine. Add the capsicum and pine nuts, and season with salt and pepper.
3 Remove the woody ends from the asparagus (hold each spear at both ends and bend gently—the woody end will snap off at its natural breaking point). Plunge the asparagus into a large frying pan of boiling water and cook for 3 minutes, or until just tender. Drain and plunge into a bowl of iced water, then drain again and gently pat dry with paper towels.
4 Arrange the asparagus on a large serving platter and spoon the dressing over the top. Garnish with the black olives and perhaps a few lemon wedges to squeeze over the top.

NUTRITION PER SERVE
Protein 4 g; Fat 25 g; Carbohydrate 5 g; Dietary Fibre 3 g; Cholesterol 0 mg; 1100 kJ (260 Cal)

Grill the capsicum pieces until the skin blackens and blisters.

Add the diced capsicum and pine nuts to the other dressing ingredients.

Cook the asparagus in boiling water, then plunge into cold water and pat dry with paper towels.

HERBED FETA SALAD

Preparation time: 20 minutes +
 30 minutes marinating
Total cooking time: 10 minutes
Serves 8

2 slices thick white bread
200 g (6¹/₂ oz) feta cheese
1 clove garlic, crushed
1 tablespoon chopped fresh marjoram
1 tablespoon snipped chives
1 tablespoon chopped fresh basil

2 tablespoons white wine vinegar
¹/₃ cup (80 ml/2³/₄ fl oz) olive oil
1 red coral lettuce
1 green mignonette or oak leaf lettuce

1 Preheat the oven to 180°C (350°F/
Gas 4). Remove the crusts from the
bread and cut the bread into small
cubes. Place on an oven tray in a
single layer and bake for 10 minutes,
until crisp and lightly golden. Transfer
to a bowl and cool completely.
2 Cut the feta into small cubes and
put in a bowl. Put the garlic, marjoram,

chives, basil, vinegar and oil in a
screw-top jar and shake well. Pour
over the feta and cover with plastic
wrap. Leave for at least 30 minutes,
stirring occasionally.
3 Tear the lettuce into large pieces
and put in a serving bowl. Add the feta
with the dressing and bread cubes and
toss the salad well.

NUTRITION PER SERVE
Protein 6 g; Fat 16 g; Carbohydrate 4 g;
Dietary Fibre 1 g; Cholesterol 17 mg;
750 kJ (180 cal)

Remove the crusts from the bread and then cut it
into small cubes.

Cut the feta into cubes and then pour the
dressing over and leave to marinate.

Add the bread cubes to the salad leaves and
marinated feta.

TOMATO, HALOUMI AND SPINACH SALAD

Preparation time: 15 minutes +
  2 hours marinating
Total cooking time: 1 hour
Serves 4

200 g (6¹/₂ oz) haloumi cheese
¹/₄ cup (60 ml/2 fl oz) olive oil
2 cloves garlic, crushed
1 tablespoon chopped fresh oregano
1 tablespoon chopped fresh marjoram
8 Roma (egg) tomatoes, halved
1 small red onion, cut into 8 wedges
  with base intact

¹/₄ cup (60 ml/2 fl oz) olive oil, extra
2 tablespoons balsamic vinegar
150 g (5 oz) baby English spinach
  leaves

1 Cut the haloumi into 1 cm (¹/₂ inch) slices lengthways and put in a shallow dish. Mix together the oil, garlic and herbs and pour over the haloumi. Marinate, covered, for 1–2 hours.
2 Preheat the oven to moderately hot 200°C (400°F/Gas 6). Place the tomato and onion in a single layer in a roasting tin, drizzle with 2 tablespoons of the extra olive oil and 1 tablespoon of the vinegar and sprinkle with salt and cracked black pepper. Bake for

50–60 minutes, or until golden.
3 Meanwhile, heat a non-stick frying pan over medium heat. Drain the haloumi and cook for 1 minute each side, or until golden brown.
4 Divide the spinach leaves among four serving plates and top with the tomato and onion. Whisk together the remaining olive oil and balsamic vinegar in a small bowl and drizzle over the salad. Top with the haloumi.

NUTRITION PER SERVE
Protein 14 g; Fat 27 g; Carbohydrate 6.5 g;
Dietary Fibre 4 g; Cholesterol 26 mg;
1333 kJ (320 Cal)

Cut the onion into eight wedges, keeping the base intact.

Arrange the tomatoes and onion in a single layer in a roasting tin and bake until golden.

Drain the marinated haloumi and cook for a minute on each side, until golden brown.

COCONUT PRAWN SALAD

Preparation time: 35 minutes +
    30 minutes refrigeration
Total cooking time: 30 minutes
Serves 4 as an entrée

24 raw king prawns, peeled and
    deveined, with tails left intact
plain flour, to coat
1 egg
1 tablespoon milk
1 cup (60 g/2 oz) shredded coconut
1/2 cup (25 g/3/4 oz) chopped fresh
    coriander leaves
1 litre (4 cups) oil
300 g (10 oz) red Asian shallots,
    chopped
2 cloves garlic, finely chopped
2 teaspoons finely chopped ginger
1 red chilli, seeds and membrane
    removed, thinly sliced
1 teaspoon ground turmeric
270 ml (91/2 fl oz) coconut cream
2 kaffir lime leaves, thinly sliced
2 teaspoons lime juice
2 teaspoons palm sugar
3 teaspoons fish sauce
1 tablespoon chopped fresh coriander
    leaves, extra
150 g (5 oz) mixed lettuce leaves

1 Holding the prawns by their tails,
coat them in flour, then dip them into
the combined egg and milk and then
in the combined coconut and
coriander. Refrigerate for 30 minutes.
2 Heat 21/2 tablespoons of the oil in a
saucepan and cook the shallots, garlic,
ginger, chilli and turmeric over
medium heat for 3–5 minutes, or until
fragrant. Add the cream, lime leaves,
lime juice, sugar and fish sauce. Bring
to the boil, then reduce the heat and
simmer for 2–3 minutes. Keep warm.
3 Heat the left over oil in a frying pan
and cook the prawns in batches for
3–5 minutes, or until golden. Drain on
paper towels and season with salt.
4 Add the extra coriander to the
dressing. Divide the lettuce, prawns
and dressing among four bowls.

NUTRITION PER SERVE
Protein 7.5 g; Fat 47 g; Carbohydrate 12 g;
Dietary Fibre 5 g; Cholesterol 55 mg;
2060 kJ (490 Cal)

Peel and devein the prawns, keeping the
tails intact.

Dip the floured prawns into the egg, then in the
coriander mixture.

Simmer the chilli dressing until it becomes
quite thick.

Cook the prawns in batches until golden, then
drain on paper towels.

SMOKED SALMON AND ROCKET SALAD

Preparation time: 20 minutes
Total cooking time: Nil
Serves 4

DRESSING
1 tablespoon extra virgin olive oil
2 tablespoons balsamic vinegar

150 g (5 oz) rocket leaves
1 avocado
250 g (8 oz) smoked salmon
325 g (11 oz) jar marinated goat's
    cheese, drained and crumbled
2 tablespoons roasted hazelnuts,
    coarsely chopped

1 For the dressing, thoroughly whisk
together the oil and vinegar in a bowl.
Season, to taste. Trim long stems from
the rocket, rinse, pat dry and gently
toss in a bowl with the dressing.
2 Cut the avocado in half lengthways,
then cut each half lengthways into
6 wedges. Discard the skin and place
3 wedges on each serving plate and
arrange a pile of rocket over the top.
3 Drape pieces of salmon over the
rocket. Scatter the cheese and nuts
over the top and season with ground
black pepper. Serve immediately.

NUTRITION PER SERVE
Protein 31.5 g; Fat 40.5 g; Carbohydrate
1.5 g; Dietary Fibre 2 g; Cholesterol
67.5 mg; 2065 kJ (490 Cal)

SUGGESTED FISH: A whole smoked
trout can be used instead of the
salmon. Peel, remove the bones, then
break the flesh into bite-sized pieces.

Drain the goat's cheese and crumble into smallish
pieces.

Toss the rocket with the dressing in a bowl until
well coated.

Cut each avocado half lengthways into
six wedges.

SNOW PEA SALAD

Preparation time: 10 minutes
Total cooking time: Nil
Serves 8

150 g (5 oz) snow peas
250 g (8 oz) fresh asparagus
2 carrots, peeled
425 g (14 oz) can baby corn, drained
230 g (7½ oz) can bamboo shoots,
    drained

DRESSING
3 tablespoons vegetable oil
3 teaspoons sesame oil
1 tablespoon soy sauce

1 Trim the snow peas and cut in half.
Snap the woody ends from the
asparagus and cut into short lengths.
Cut the carrots into matchsticks.
2 Put the snow peas and asparagus in
a heatproof bowl and cover with
boiling water. Leave for 1 minute, then
drain and plunge into iced water.
Drain and dry on paper towels.
3 Combine the snow peas, asparagus,
carrots, corn and bamboo shoots in a
serving bowl. To make the dressing,
put the oils and sauce in a small screw-
top jar and shake well to combine.
Pour over the salad and toss well.

NUTRITION PER SERVE
Protein 3 g; Fat 10 g; Carbohydrate 12 g;
Dietary Fibre 4 g; Cholesterol 0 mg;
603 kJ (144 cal)

NOTE: Sesame oil is a very strongly
flavoured oil and should be used
sparingly as its flavour tends to
dominate. The darker the oil, the
stronger the flavour.

Cut all the vegetables into similar-sized strips and
pieces so the salad is balanced.

Drain the snow peas and asparagus and then pat
dry on paper towels.

Combine all the dressing ingredients in a screw-
top jar, then pour over the salad.

MEXICANA SALAD

Preparation time: 40 minutes +
  overnight standing
Total cooking time: 1 hour
Serves 10–12

250 g (8 oz) black-eyed beans
250 g (8 oz) red kidney beans
500 g (1 lb) sweet potato
1 large red onion, chopped
1 large green capsicum,
  chopped
3 ripe tomatoes, chopped
1/4 cup (15 g/1/2 oz) chopped basil
3 flour tortillas
1 tablespoon oil
2 tablespoons grated Parmesan
1/4 cup (60 g/2 oz) sour cream

DRESSING
1 clove garlic, crushed
1 tablespoon lime juice
2 tablespoons olive oil

GUACAMOLE
3 avocados
2 tablespoons lemon juice
1 clove garlic, crushed
1 small red onion, chopped
1 small red chilli, chopped
1/4 cup (60 g/2 oz) sour cream
2 tablespoons hot ready-made taco
  sauce

1 Soak the beans in a large bowl of cold water overnight. Drain and cook in a large pan of rapidly boiling water for 30 minutes, or until just tender. Skim off any scum that appears on the surface during cooking. Do not overcook or they will become mushy. Drain and set aside to cool.
2 Chop the sweet potato into large pieces and cook in boiling water until tender. Drain and combine with the onion, capsicum, tomato and beans. Stir in the basil.
3 To make the dressing, shake the ingredients in a jar until combined. Pour over the salad and toss to coat.
4 Preheat the oven to moderate 180°C (350°F/Gas 4). Using a small knife, cut cactus shapes or large triangles out of the tortillas, brush lightly with the oil and sprinkle with Parmesan. Bake for 5–10 minutes, or until they are crisp and golden.
5 To make the guacamole, mash the avocados with the lemon juice. Add the garlic, onion, chilli, sour cream and taco sauce and mix well.
6 Pile the guacamole in the centre of the salad, top with the sour cream and arrange the cactus shapes on top.

NUTRITION PER SERVE (12)
Protein 15 g; Fat 25 g; Carbohydrate 40 g;
Dietary Fibre 10 g; Cholesterol 15 mg;
1735 kJ (415 Cal)

Combine the sweet potato with the onion, capsicum, tomato and beans.

Using a small sharp knife, cut cactus shapes out of the tortillas.

WARM MARINATED MUSHROOM SALAD

Preparation time: 25 minutes +
  20 minutes marinating
Total cooking time: 5 minutes
Serves 4

750 g (1½ lb) mixed mushrooms
    (such as baby button, oyster,
    Swiss brown, shiitake and enoki)
2 cloves garlic, finely chopped
½ teaspoon green peppercorns,
    crushed
⅓ cup (80 ml/2¾ fl oz) olive oil
⅓ cup (80 ml/2¾ fl oz) orange juice
250 g (8 oz) salad leaves, watercress
    or baby spinach leaves
1 teaspoon finely grated orange rind

1 Trim the mushroom stems and wipe the mushrooms with a damp paper towel. Cut any large mushrooms in half. Mix together the garlic, peppercorns, olive oil and orange juice. Pour over the mushrooms and marinate for about 20 minutes.
2 Arrange the salad leaves in a serving dish.
3 Drain the mushrooms, reserving the marinade. Cook the flat and button mushrooms on a hot, lightly oiled barbecue grill or flatplate for about 2 minutes. Add the softer mushrooms and cook for 1 minute, or until they just soften.
4 Scatter the mushrooms over the salad leaves and drizzle with the marinade. Sprinkle with orange rind and season well.

NUTRITION PER SERVE
Protein 10 g; Fat 15 g; Carbohydrate 5 g;
Dietary Fibre 5 g; Cholesterol 0 mg;
790 kJ (190 cal)

Trim the mushroom stems and wipe clean with paper towel. Cut any large mushrooms in half.

Mix together the garlic, peppercorns, olive oil and orange juice and pour over the mushrooms.

Add the softer mushrooms to the barbecue and just cook for 1 minute.

ROASTED FENNEL AND ORANGE SALAD

Preparation time: 30 minutes
Total cooking time: 1 hour
Serves 4

8 baby fennel bulbs
100 ml (3½ fl oz) olive oil
1 teaspoon sea salt
2 oranges
1 tablespoon lemon juice
1 red onion, halved and thinly sliced
100 g (3½ oz) Kalamata olives
2 tablespoons chopped fresh mint
1 tablespoon roughly chopped fresh
    flat-leaf parsley

1 Preheat the oven to moderately hot 200°C (400°F/Gas 6). Trim and reserve the fennel fronds. Remove the stalks and cut a slice off the base of each fennel about 5 mm (¼ inch) thick. Slice each fennel into 6 wedges. Place in a baking dish and drizzle with ¼ cup (60 ml/2 fl oz) of the oil. Add the salt and plenty of pepper to taste. Bake for 40–60 minutes, or until the fennel is tender and slightly caramelised. Cool.
2 Cut a slice off the top and bottom of each orange. Using a small sharp knife, slice off the skin and pith, following the curves of the orange. Remove as much pith as possible. Slice down the side of a segment between the flesh and the membrane. Repeat with the other side and lift the segment out. Do this over a bowl to catch the segments and juices. Repeat with each segment. Squeeze any juice from the membrane. Drain and reserve the juice.
3 Whisk the remaining olive oil into the orange juice and the lemon juice until emulsified. Season well. Combine the orange segments, onion and olives in a serving dish, pour on half the dressing and add half the mint. Mix well. Top with the fennel, drizzle with the remaining dressing, and scatter with the parsley and the remaining mint. Roughly chop the reserved fronds and scatter over the salad.

NUTRITION PER SERVE
Protein 5 g; Fat 25 g; Carbohydrate 19 g;
Dietary Fibre 15 g; Cholesterol 0 mg;
1339 kJ (320 Cal)

Use a sharp knife to slice each of the baby fennels into wedges.

Bake the fennel until tender and slightly caramelised.

Remove the orange skin and pith with a small sharp knife.

Cut the orange between the flesh and the membrane to remove the segments.

JAPANESE SALAD ON RICE TIMBALES

Preparation time: 25 minutes
+ 15 minutes standing
Total cooking time: 15 minutes
Serves 6

SUSHI RICE
2 cups (440 g/14 oz) short- or
    medium-grain rice
1 1/2 tablespoons sugar
1/2 cup (125 ml/4 fl oz) Japanese
    rice vinegar
2 tablespoons mirin

WASABI MAYONNAISE
1 cup (250 g/8 oz) whole-egg
    mayonnaise
2 tablespoons Japanese rice vinegar
3 teaspoons wasabi paste

3 sheets nori
300 g (10 oz) good-quality salmon,
    very thinly sliced
1 avocado
toasted black sesame seeds,
    for serving
pickled ginger, finely sliced,
    for serving
Japanese soy sauce, for serving

1 Rinse the rice under cold water until the water runs clear. Place in a saucepan with 2 1/2 cups (625 ml/ 20 fl oz) water, cover, bring to the boil, then reduce the heat and simmer for 8–10 minutes, or until all the water is absorbed. Remove from the heat and leave, covered, for 15 minutes, or until cooked through.
2 Meanwhile, put the sugar, vinegar, mirin and 1/2 teaspoon salt in a small saucepan and stir over medium heat for 2–3 minutes, or until the sugar has

dissolved. Lay the rice out on a flat non-metallic tray, pour the vinegar mixture over the top and stir through.
3 For the wasabi mayonnaise, mix all the ingredients together in a bowl.
4 Cut circles from the nori to fit the bases of six 1 cup (250 ml/8 fl oz) ramekins. Cover the base of each ramekin with 50 g (1 3/4 oz) salmon. Spread 2 teaspoons of the wasabi mayonnaise over each salmon layer. Top with nori, then fill each ramekin three quarters full using about 2/3 cup

(125 g/4 oz) sushi rice. Refrigerate until just before serving.
5 Cut the avocado into cubes. Dip a knife in hot water and run around the ramekin edges to loosen the rice. Turn out, top with avocado and sprinkle with sesame seeds. Serve with the mayonnaise, ginger and soy sauce.

NUTRITION PER SERVE
Protein 20.5 g; Fat 25.5 g; Carbohydrate 71.5 g; Dietary Fibre 3 g; Cholesterol 37.5 mg; 2495 kJ (595 Cal)

Remove from the heat when all the water is absorbed and holes form on top.

Using the ramekins as a guide, cut circles from the nori with a sharp knife.

To release the rice, dip a knife in hot water and run it around the edges.

PEAR AND WALNUT SALAD WITH LIME VINAIGRETTE

Preparation time: 25 minutes
Total cooking time: 20 minutes
Serves 4

1 small baguette, cut into 16 thin
    slices
soy bean oil, for brushing
1 clove garlic, cut in half
1 cup (100 g/3¹/₂ oz) walnuts
200 g (6¹/₂ oz) soy cheese
400 g (13 oz) mesclun leaves
2 pears, cut into 2 cm (³/₄ inch) cubes,
    mixed with 2 tablespoons lime juice

LIME VINAIGRETTE
3 tablespoons soy bean oil
¹/₄ cup (60 ml/2 fl oz) lime juice
2 tablespoons raspberry vinegar

1 Preheat the oven to moderate 180°C (350°F/Gas 4). Brush the baguette slices with a little oil, rub with the cut side of the garlic, then place on a baking tray. Bake for 10 minutes, or until crisp and golden. Place the walnuts on a baking tray and roast for 5–8 minutes, or until slightly browned—shake the tray to ensure even colouring. Allow to cool for 5 minutes.
2 To make the lime vinaigrette, whisk together the oil, lime juice, raspberry vinegar, 1 teaspoon salt and ¹/₂ teaspoon freshly ground black pepper in a small bowl. Set aside until ready to use.
3 Spread some of the soy cheese on each crouton, then cook under a hot grill (broiler) for 2–3 minutes, or until hot.
4 Place the mesclun, pears and walnuts in a bowl, add the vinaigrette and toss through. Divide the salad among four serving bowls and serve with the soy cheese croutons.

NUTRITION PER SERVE
Protein 24 g; Fat 60 g; Carbohydrate 40 g;
Dietary Fibre 7 g; Cholesterol 0 mg;
3310 kJ (790 Cal)

Rub each slice of baguette with a cut piece of garlic.

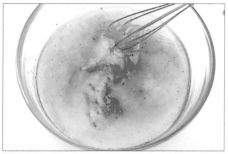
Whisk together the soy bean oil, lime juice, raspberry vinegar, salt and pepper.

Place the soy cheese-topped croutons on a baking tray and grill until hot.

WARM CHICKPEA AND SILVERBEET SALAD WITH SUMAC

Preparation time: 30 minutes
  + overnight soaking
Total cooking time: 2 hours
Serves 4

250 g (8 oz) dried chickpeas
1/2 cup (125 ml/4 fl oz) olive oil
1 onion, cut into thin wedges
2 tomatoes
1 teaspoon sugar
1/4 teaspoon ground cinnamon
2 cloves garlic, chopped
1.5 kg (3 lb) silverbeet

3 tablespoons chopped fresh mint
2–3 tablespoons lemon juice
1 1/2 tablespoons ground sumac
  (see NOTE)

1 Place the chickpeas in a large bowl, cover with water and leave to soak overnight. Drain and place in a large saucepan. Cover with water and bring to the boil, then simmer for 1 3/4 hours, or until tender. Drain.
2 Heat the oil in a frying pan, add the onion and cook over low heat for 3–4 minutes, or until soft and just starting to brown. Cut the tomatoes in half, remove the seeds and dice the flesh. Add to the pan with the sugar, cinnamon and garlic, and cook

for 2–3 minutes, or until softened.
3 Wash the silverbeet and dry with paper towel. Trim the stems and finely shred the leaves. Add to the tomato mixture with the chickpeas and cook for 3–4 minutes, or until the silverbeet wilts. Add the mint, lemon juice and sumac, season, and cook for 1 minute. Serve immediately.

NUTRITION PER SERVE
Protein 18 g; Fat 34 g; Carbohydrate 30 g;
Dietary Fibre 20 g; Cholesterol 0 mg;
2080 kJ (497 Cal)

NOTE: Sumac is available from Middle Eastern speciality shops.

Scoop the seeds out of the halved tomatoes with a teaspoon.

Add the tomato, sugar, cinnamon and garlic to the pan and cook until soft.

Add the silverbeet and chickpeas and cook until the spinach is wilted.

EGGPLANT, CAPSICUM, PESTO AND GOAT'S MILK CHEESE SALAD STACK

Preparation time: 20 minutes +
  30 minutes standing
Total cooking time: 15 minutes
Serves 4 as an entrée

1 kg (2 lb) eggplant, cut into twelve
  1.5 cm (5/8 inch) slices (ends
  discarded)
1 large red capsicum
olive oil, for pan-frying
1 cup (45 g/1 1/2 oz) rocket leaves
100 g (3 1/2 oz) goat's milk cheese
shredded rocket or basil, to garnish
balsamic vinegar, to serve (optional)
olive oil, to serve (optional)

PESTO
1 1/2 cups (75 g/2 1/2 oz) firmly packed
  fresh basil
2 cloves garlic
2 tablespoons pine nuts, toasted
1 tablespoon lemon juice
1 1/2 tablespoons grated Parmesan
1/2 cup (125 ml/4 fl oz) olive oil

1 Rub salt generously into the eggplant slices, then sit in a colander for 30 minutes. Rinse under cold water and pat the eggplant dry.
2 Cut the capsicum into large pieces, removing the seeds and membrane. Place, skin-side-up, under a hot grill (broiler) until the skin blackens and blisters. Cool in a plastic bag, then peel away the skin. Slice thinly.
3 To make the pesto, combine the basil, garlic, pine nuts, lemon juice and Parmesan in a food processor and process until finely minced. With the motor running, slowly pour in the oil and blend until smooth.

4 Lightly cover the base of a frying pan with oil and heat over medium heat. Add the eggplant in batches and cook both sides until golden, adding more oil as needed. Drain on crumpled paper towels and keep warm.
5 To assemble, lay a few rocket leaves on a plate. Place one slice of eggplant on the rocket, then top with some more rocket leaves, a heaped teaspoon of pesto, one eighth of the capsicum and one eighth of the goat's milk cheese. Repeat, making two

layers and finish with a final slice of eggplant. Dollop some pesto on the top of the stack, sprinkle with shredded rocket or basil and season with pepper. Repeat, making three more stacks. Drizzle balsamic vinegar and olive oil around the plate, if desired. Serve immediately.

NUTRITION PER SERVE
Protein 12 g; Fat 55 g; Carbohydrate 8.5 g; Dietary Fibre 7 g; Cholesterol 24 mg; 2397 kJ (573 Cal)

Cook the capsicum under a hot grill until the skin blackens and blisters.

Add the olive oil and blend until the pesto is smooth.

Cook both sides of the eggplant until golden, then drain on paper towels.

WILD MUSHROOM SALAD

Preparation time: 15 minutes
Total cooking time: 15 minutes
Serves 4

100 g (3½ oz) hazelnuts
1 mizuna lettuce
90 g (3 oz) baby curly endive
60 g (2 oz) baby English spinach
2 tablespoons hazelnut oil
2 tablespoons light olive oil
500 g (1 lb) wild mushrooms
    (enoki, shimeji, Shiitake, oyster)
150 g (5 oz) strong blue cheese,
    crumbled

TOMATO MUSTARD VINAIGRETTE
½ cup (125 ml/4 fl oz) light olive oil
2 tablespoons tarragon vinegar
1 teaspoon tomato mustard

1 Preheat the oven to moderate 180°C (350°F/Gas 4). Put the hazelnuts on a baking tray and cook for 10 minutes, shaking the tray occasionally. Remove from the oven, cool, and remove the skins by rubbing the nuts together in a tea towel. Coarsely chop the nuts.
2 Remove the tough lower stems from the mizuna and endive, and tear the larger leaves into bite-sized pieces. Wash the mizuna, endive and spinach under cold water, dry completely and refrigerate until well chilled.
3 To make the vinaigrette, whisk the ingredients together and season well.
4 Heat the oils in a frying pan and sauté the mushrooms for 3–4 minutes, or until beginning to soften. Remove from the heat and cool slightly, then stir in the vinaigrette. Arrange the salad greens on serving plates. Spoon the mushrooms over the top and sprinkle with cheese and hazelnuts.

NUTRITION PER SERVE
Protein 10 g; Fat 75 g; Carbohydrate 20 g;
Dietary Fibre 4 g; Cholesterol 40 mg;
3375 kJ (805 Cal)

NOTE: Chestnut mushrooms or chanterelles can also be used. Pink oyster mushrooms, if available, make this salad look particularly attractive.

Rub the hazelnuts together in a tea towel to remove the skins.

Remove the tough lower stems from the baby curly endive.

Sauté the mushrooms until they are just beginning to soften.

LEEK AND CAPER SALAD

Preparation time: 20 minutes
Total cooking time: 20 minutes
Serves 6

5 leeks, white part only
1/3 cup (80 ml/2³/4 fl oz) olive oil
2 tablespoons sherry vinegar
2 tablespoons baby capers, rinsed

1 Cut the leeks in half lengthways and wash thoroughly under cold running water. Cut them into 5 cm (2 inch) lengths, then cut in half again lengthways. Heat the oil in a large heavy-based pan, add the leeks and stir until coated with the oil. Cover and cook over low heat for 15–20 minutes, or until the leeks are soft and tender (but don't let them brown or burn). Cool for 10 minutes.

2 Stir through the vinegar and season to taste with salt and pepper. Transfer to a serving dish and scatter with the baby capers (if baby capers are unavailable, use chopped ordinary-sized capers).

NUTRITION PER SERVE
Protein 1.5 g; Fat 13 g; Carbohydrate 2.5 g;
Dietary Fibre 2 g; Cholesterol 0 mg;
550 kJ (130 Cal)

Trim the leeks and wash them thoroughly under cold running water.

Add the leeks to the pan and stir until they are covered with the oil.

Add the vinegar to the cooled leeks and stir until they are well coated.

main meal salads

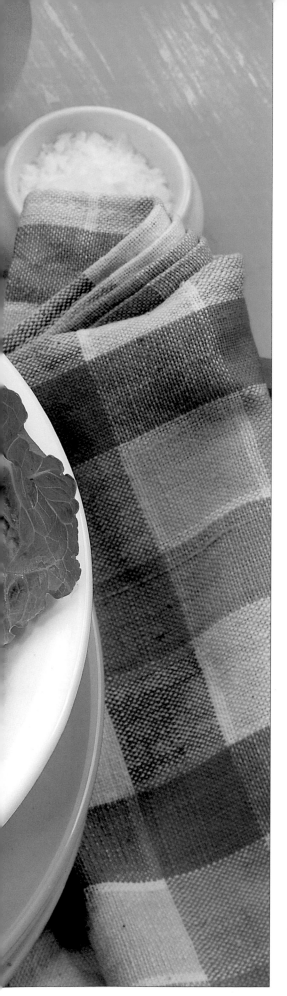

SMOKED CHICKEN CAESAR SALAD

Preparation time: 25 minutes
Total cooking time: 15 minutes
Serves 4

GARLIC CROUTONS
1 thin baguette
45 g (1¹/₂ oz) unsalted butter
¹/₂ cup (125 ml/4 fl oz) olive oil
4 cloves garlic, crushed

1 cos lettuce, tough outer leaves
    discarded
1 large smoked chicken (about
    950 g/1 lb 14 oz)
1¹/₂ cups (150 g/5 oz) Parmesan
    shavings

DRESSING
2 eggs
2 cloves garlic, crushed
2 tablespoons lemon juice
2 teaspoons Dijon mustard
45 g (1¹/₂ oz) can anchovy fillets,
    drained
1 cup (250 ml/8 fl oz) olive oil
¹/₄ teaspoon salt
1 teaspoon freshly ground black
    pepper

1 To make the garlic croutons, slice
the baguette diagonally into 1 cm
(¹/₂ inch) thick slices. Melt the butter
and olive oil in a large frying pan over
moderate heat. Stir in the crushed
garlic. Fry the bread slices, a few at a
time, until golden. Remove from the
pan and drain on paper towels.
2 Separate the lettuce leaves, wash
and dry thoroughly. Tear the larger
leaves into pieces and refrigerate until
well chilled. Cut the chicken into bite-
sized chunks. Refrigerate while
preparing the dressing.
3 To make the dressing, blend or
process the eggs, garlic, lemon juice,
mustard and anchovies. With the
motor running, gradually pour in the
oil in a thin stream and process until
thick. Season with the salt and pepper.
4 In a large bowl, combine the torn
lettuce leaves, chicken, about half of
the croutons and half the Parmesan.
Add the dressing and toss well.
Arrange 2–3 whole lettuce leaves in
each individual serving bowl, spoon in
the salad and sprinkle with the
remaining croutons and Parmesan.
Season liberally with freshly ground
black pepper and serve immediately.

NUTRITION PER SERVE
Protein 45 g; Fat 120 g; Carbohydrate 10 g;
Dietary Fibre 2 g; Cholesterol 235 mg;
5350 kJ (1275 Cal)

Roughly chop the smoked chicken meat into
bite-sized chunks.

Process the eggs, garlic, lemon juice, mustard
and anchovies.

TANDOORI CHICKEN SALAD

Preparation time: 20 minutes
  + overnight marinating
Total cooking time: 15 minutes
Serves 4

4 chicken breast fillets
2–3 tablespoons tandoori paste
200 g (6^{1}/$_{2}$ oz) thick plain yoghurt
1 tablespoon lemon juice
^{1}/$_{2}$ cup (15 g/^{1}/$_{2}$ oz) fresh coriander
  leaves
^{1}/$_{2}$ cup (60 g/2 oz) slivered almonds,
  toasted
snow pea sprouts, to serve

CUCUMBER AND YOGHURT DRESSING
1 Lebanese cucumber, grated
200 g (6^{1}/$_{2}$ oz) thick plain yoghurt
1 tablespoon chopped fresh mint
2 teaspoons lemon juice

1 Cut the chicken breast fillets into thick strips. Combine the tandoori paste, yoghurt and lemon juice in a large bowl, add the chicken strips and toss to coat well. Refrigerate and leave to marinate overnight.
2 To make the dressing, put the grated cucumber in a medium bowl. Add the yoghurt, chopped mint and lemon juice, and stir until well combined. Refrigerate until needed.
3 Heat a large non-stick frying pan, add the marinated chicken in batches and cook, turning frequently, until cooked through. Cool and place in a large bowl. Add the coriander leaves and toasted almonds, and toss until well combined. Serve on a bed of snow pea sprouts, with the dressing served separately.

NUTRITION PER SERVE
Protein 35 g; Fat 15 g; Carbohydrate 7 g;
Dietary Fibre 2 g; Cholesterol 70 mg;
1230 kJ (290 Cal)

NOTE: The quality of the tandoori paste used will determine the flavour and look of the chicken. There are many home-made varieties available from supermarkets and delicatessens.

Combine the tandoori paste with the yoghurt and lemon juice.

Using a metal grater, coarsely grate the unpeeled Lebanese cucumber.

Cook the marinated chicken strips in batches, turning frequently.

QUICK BEEF AND NOODLE SALAD

Preparation time: 15 minutes
Total cooking time: 10 minutes
Serves 4

500 g (1 lb) rump steak
1 tablespoon peanut oil
2 tablespoons oyster sauce
2 teaspoons mild curry powder
1 tablespoon soft brown sugar
1 small Lebanese cucumber, sliced
1 red onion, sliced
1 red capsicum, cut into thin strips
1 small red chilli, seeded and chopped
1/4 cup (15 g/1/2 oz) chopped fresh mint
1/3 cup (60 g/2 oz) chopped unsalted peanuts or cashews
500 g (1 lb) Hokkien noodles

DRESSING
1/2 cup (125 ml/4 fl oz) rice vinegar (see NOTE)
2 tablespoons fish sauce
1/4 cup (60 g/2 oz) caster sugar
2 teaspoons finely chopped fresh ginger
1 small red chilli, seeded and chopped
1 tablespoon chopped fresh coriander leaves

1 Remove all visible fat from the meat. Combine the peanut oil, oyster sauce, curry powder and brown sugar in a small bowl.

2 Heat a wok over medium heat. Add the steak and cook for 6–8 minutes, turning and basting with half the sauce during cooking. Remove the steak from the wok.

3 To make the dressing, whisk together all the ingredients.

4 Place the cucumber, onion, capsicum and chilli in a large bowl. Add the mint and nuts. Thinly slice the meat, add to the bowl with the dressing and lightly toss to combine. If you have time, leave for a few minutes to marinate.

5 Place the noodles in the same wok and stir-fry over medium heat for 1–2 minutes. Stir in the remaining basting sauce and toss until heated through. Divide the noodles among serving bowls and top with the salad. Serve immediately.

NUTRITION PER SERVE
Protein 50 g; Fat 17 g; Carbohydrate 115 g; Dietary Fibre 5.5 g; Cholesterol 105 mg; 3405 kJ (815 Cal)

NOTE: Rice vinegar is available in Asian grocery stores.

While you cook the steak, turn it and baste often with the sauce.

Place the cucumber, onion, capsicum and chilli in a large bowl and add the mint and nuts.

Stir the remaining basting sauce into the noodles in the wok.

INSALATA DI FRUTTI DI MARE (Seafood salad)

Preparation time: 45 minutes
    + 40 minutes marinating
Total cooking time: 10 minutes
Serves 4

500 g (1 lb) small calamari
1 kg (2 lb) large clams
1 kg (2 lb) black mussels
500 g (1 lb) raw medium prawns,
    peeled and deveined, tails intact
5 tablespoons finely chopped fresh
    flat-leaf parsley

DRESSING
2 tablespoons lemon juice
1/3 cup (80 ml/2³/4 fl oz) olive oil
1 garlic clove, crushed

1 Grasp the body of the calamari in one hand and the head and tentacles in the other. Gently pull apart to separate. Cut the tentacles from the head by cutting below the eyes. Discard the head. Push out the beak and discard. Pull the quill from inside the body of the calamari and discard. Under cold running water, pull away all the skin (the flaps can be used). Rinse well, then slice the calamari into 7 mm (1/4 inch) rings.

2 Scrub the clams and mussels and remove the beards. Discard any that are cracked or don't close when tapped. Rinse under cold running water. Fill a large saucepan with 2 cm (3/4 inch) water, add the clams and mussels, cover, bring to the boil and cook for 4–5 minutes, or until the shells open. Remove, reserving the liquid. Discard any that do not open. Remove the mussels and clams from their shells and place in a large bowl.

3 Pour 1 litre (32 fl oz) water into the pan, bring to the boil and add the prawns and calamari. Cook for 3–4 minutes, or until the prawns turn pink and the calamari is tender. Drain and add to the clams and mussels.

4 To make the dressing, combine the lemon juice, olive oil and garlic in a small bowl and whisk together. Season with salt and freshly ground black pepper. Pour the dressing over the seafood, add 4 tablespoons of the parsley and toss to coat. Adjust the seasoning if necessary. Cover and marinate in the refrigerator for 30–40 minutes to allow the flavours to develop. Sprinkle with the remaining parsley and serve with slices of fresh crusty bread.

NUTRITION PER SERVE
Protein 76 g; Fat 25 g; Carbohydrate 2 g;
Dietary Fibre 0 g; Cholesterol 550 mg;
3420 kJ (815 Cal)

Remove the transparent quill from inside the body of the calamari.

Gently pull the mussels and clams out of their shells.

WARM LAMB SALAD

Preparation time: 15 minutes
  + 3 hours refrigeration
Total cooking time: 15 minutes
Serves 4–6

2 tablespoons red curry paste
1/4 cup (15 g/1/2 oz) chopped fresh
  coriander leaves
1 tablespoon finely grated fresh ginger
3–4 tablespoons peanut oil
750 g (11/2 lb) lamb fillets, thinly sliced
200 g (61/2 oz) snow peas
600 g (11/4 lb) packet thick fresh rice
  noodles
1 red capsicum, thinly sliced
1 Lebanese cucumber, thinly sliced
6 spring onions, thinly sliced

MINT DRESSING
11/2 tablespoons peanut oil
1/4 cup (60 ml/2 fl oz) lime juice
2 tablespoons soft brown sugar
3 teaspoons fish sauce
3 teaspoons soy sauce
1/3 cup (20 g/3/4 oz) chopped fresh
  mint leaves
1 clove garlic, crushed

1 Combine the curry paste, coriander, ginger and 2 tablespoons oil in a bowl. Add the lamb and coat well. Cover and refrigerate for 2–3 hours.
2 Steam or boil the snow peas until just tender, refresh under cold water and drain.
3 Cover the noodles with boiling water. Leave for 5 minutes, or until tender, and drain.

4 To make the dressing, put all the ingredients in a jar and shake well.
5 Heat a wok until very hot, add 1 tablespoon oil and swirl to coat. Add half the lamb and stir-fry for 5 minutes, or until tender. Repeat with the remaining lamb, using more oil if needed.
6 Place the lamb, snow peas, noodles, capsicum, cucumber and spring onion in a large bowl, drizzle with the dressing and toss before serving.

NUTRITION PER SERVE (6)
Protein 32 g; Fat 20 g; Carbohydrate 33 g;
Dietary Fibre 3 g; Cholesterol 83 mg;
1850 kJ (442 Cal)

Mix together the curry paste, coriander, ginger and 2 tablespoons oil.

Leave the thick fresh rice noodles in boiling water until they are tender, then drain.

Put all the dressing ingredients in a screw-top jar and shake well to mix them.

PRAWN AND PASTA SALAD

Preparation time: 15 minutes
Total cooking time: 15 minutes
Serves 4

DRESSING
1/3 cup (80 ml/2³/4 fl oz) olive oil
1¹/2 tablespoons white wine vinegar
1¹/2 tablespoons pine nuts,
    toasted
1 tablespoon roughly chopped fresh
    basil
1 tablespoon roughly chopped fresh
    flat-leaf parsley
1 clove garlic
1 tablespoon grated Parmesan
pinch of sugar

400 g (13 oz) large pasta shells
1 tablespoon olive oil, extra
500 g (1 lb) small cooked prawns
100 g (3¹/2 oz) bocconcini, thinly
    sliced
125 g (4 oz) chargrilled red capsicum,
    cut into thin strips
125 g (4 oz) cherry tomatoes, halved
fresh basil leaves, to garnish

1 For the dressing, process all the ingredients together in a blender or food processor until smooth.
2 Cook the pasta in a large pan of rapidly boiling salted water until *al dente*. Drain well, return to the pan and toss with the extra olive oil. Allow to cool.
3 Peel the prawns and gently pull out the dark vein from each prawn back, starting at the head end.
4 Put the pasta, prawns, bocconcini, capsicum and tomatoes in a serving bowl and pour on the dressing. Toss together well and garnish with basil leaves to serve.

NUTRITION PER SERVE
Protein 51 g; Fat 35 g; Carbohydrate 73 g;
Dietary Fibre 7 g; Cholesterol 257 mg;
3420 kJ (815 Cal)

Slice the chargrilled red capsicum into very thin strips.

Process all the dressing ingredients together until well blended and smooth.

Gently pull out the dark vein from the back of each peeled prawn.

CHILLI SALT SQUID AND CELLOPHANE NOODLE SALAD

Preparation time: 30 minutes +
    30 minutes soaking +
    15 minutes refrigeration
Cooking time: 10 minutes
Serves 4

DRESSING
1 tablespoon dried shrimp
2 tablespoons Chinese rice wine
2 tablespoons light soy sauce
1 tablespoon Chinese black vinegar
1 teaspoon chilli garlic sauce
2 teaspoons finely chopped ginger
2 spring onions, thinly sliced
1 teaspoon sesame oil

600 g (1 lb 5 oz) cleaned squid tubes
1/2 cup (125 ml/4 fl oz) lemon juice
250 g (8 oz) dried mung bean
    vermicelli
1 small Lebanese cucumber, seeded
    and cut into batons
90 g (3 1/4 oz) bean sprouts, trimmed
2 tablespoons chopped coriander
    leaves
1 tablespoon Sichuan peppercorns,
    dry roasted
1/4 teaspoon dried chilli flakes
2 teaspoons sea salt
1 teaspoon ground white pepper
1 teaspoon ground black pepper
1/4 cup (45 g/1 1/2 oz) rice flour
1/2 cup (60 g/2 oz) plain flour
peanut oil, to deep-fry
2 egg whites, lightly beaten
coriander leaves, to garnish

1 To make the dressing, place the dried shrimp in a small heatproof bowl, cover with boiling water and soak for 10 minutes. Drain and finely chop. Return the shrimp to the bowl, cover with the rice wine and allow to soak for a further 15 minutes. In a separate bowl, combine the soy sauce, black vinegar, chilli sauce, ginger, spring onion and sesame oil. Set aside.
2 Meanwhile, open out the squid tubes, wash and thoroughly pat dry with paper towels. With the soft inside facing upwards, score a diamond pattern using a small sharp knife, taking care not to cut through all the way. Cut the squid into 4 cm x 2.5 cm (1 1/2 inch x 1 inch) pieces, place in a flat non-metallic dish and pour the lemon juice on top. Cover with plastic wrap and marinate in the refrigerator for 15 minutes.
3 Place the noodles in a large heatproof dish, cover with boiling water and soak for 3–4 minutes, or until softened. Drain and rinse under cold running water. Drain again, then transfer to a serving bowl. Add the cucumber, bean sprouts and chopped coriander leaves.
4 Combine the dry-roasted Sichuan peppercorns, chilli flakes, sea salt, white pepper and black pepper in a mortar and pestle or spice grinder and grind to a fine powder. Transfer to a bowl with the rice and plain flours and combine thoroughly. Drain the squid and pat dry with paper towels.
5 Fill a deep heavy-based saucepan, wok or deep-fryer one-third full of oil and heat to 180°C (350°F), or until a cube of bread browns in 15 seconds. Dip the squid pieces in the egg white, then coat well in the seasoned flour. Deep-fry in batches of 5 or 6 for about 1 minute, or until lightly golden and cooked through—do not overcrowd the pan. Drain on crumpled paper towels and season to taste with salt and freshly ground black pepper.

6 To serve, add the dressing and shrimp mixture to the noodles and gently toss to combine in a large bowl. Place the squid on top of the noodles, garnish with the coriander leaves and serve immediately.

NUTRITION PER SERVE
Protein 32.5 g; Fat 9.5 g; Carbohydrate 55.5 g;
Dietary Fibre 4 g; Cholesterol 298.5 mg;
1900 kJ (455 Cal)

Once the dried shrimp have been soaked, finely chop with a sharp knife.

Score a diamond pattern onto the surface of the squid—do not cut all the way through.

Deep-fry the squid pieces until lightly golden and cooked through.

RED CURRY CHICKEN SALAD

Preparation time: 30 minutes
 + overnight marinating
Total cooking time: 20 minutes
Serves 4

500 g (1 lb) chicken thigh fillets,
   cut into thin strips
2 teaspoons Thai red curry paste
1 teaspoon chopped red chilli
1 clove garlic, crushed
1 stem lemon grass, white part only,
   finely chopped
cooking oil spray
1 red onion, thinly sliced
2 tomatoes, cut into wedges
1/2 cup (25 g/3/4 oz) chopped fresh mint
1/4 cup (15 g/1/2 oz) chopped fresh
   coriander
400 g (13 oz) mixed salad leaves
2 tablespoons roasted peanuts

DRESSING
11/2 tablespoons soft brown sugar
2 tablespoons fish sauce
2 tablespoons lime juice
2 kaffir lime leaves, shredded
2 teaspoons oil

1 Combine the chicken, curry paste,
chilli, garlic and lemon grass. Cover
and refrigerate overnight.
2 Lightly spray a non-stick frying pan
with oil and cook the chicken in
batches until tender and lightly
browned; set aside. Add the onion to
the pan and cook for 1 minute, or until
just soft. Return the chicken and any
juices to the pan and add the tomato,
mint and coriander, stirring until
heated. Set aside until just warm.
3 To make the dressing, put the sugar,
fish sauce, lime juice, lime leaves and
oil in a jug. Mix until combined. In a
large bowl, toss the chicken mixture
with the salad leaves and dressing.
Sprinkle with the peanuts to serve.

NUTRITION PER SERVE
Protein 25 g; Fat 10 g; Carbohydrate 15 g;
Dietary Fibre 2.5 g; Cholesterol 50 mg;
1050 kJ (250 cal)

Remove the fat from the chicken fillets and cut
the meat into strips.

If you find it easier, you can use your hands to
mix the chicken and marinade.

Stir the tomatoes and herbs with the chicken,
until heated through.

SALAD PASTA WRAP

Preparation time: 20 minutes
Total cooking time: 20 minutes
Serves 4

BALSAMIC SYRUP
1/3 cup (80 ml/2¾ fl oz) balsamic
    vinegar
1½ tablespoons brown sugar

1 cup (150 g/5 oz) fresh or frozen
    peas
16 asparagus spears, trimmed and
    cut into 5 cm (2 inch) lengths
2 large zucchini, cut into thin ribbons
2 fresh lasagne sheets, each sheet
    24 cm x 35 cm (9½ inch x 14 inch)
100 g (3½ oz) rocket leaves
1 cup (30 g/1 oz) fresh basil, torn
2 tablespoons extra virgin olive oil
250 g (8 oz) low-fat ricotta
150 g (5 oz) semi-dried tomatoes
Parmesan shavings, to garnish

1 To make the syrup, place the vinegar and sugar in a saucepan and stir over medium heat until the sugar dissolves. Reduce the heat and simmer for 3 minutes, or until the sauce becomes syrupy. Remove from the heat.
2 Bring a saucepan of salted water to the boil. Blanch the peas, asparagus and zucchini in separate batches until just tender, removing each batch with a slotted spoon and refreshing in cold water. Reserve the cooking liquid and return to the boil.
3 Cook the lasagne sheets in the boiling water for 1–2 minutes, or until *al dente*. Refresh in cold water and drain. Cut each in half lengthways.
4 Toss the vegetables and the rocket with the basil and olive oil. Season.
5 To assemble, place one strip of pasta on a serving plate—one-third on the centre of the plate and two-thirds overhanging one side. Place some of the salad on the centre one-third, topped with some ricotta and tomato. Season and fold over one-third of the lasagne sheet. Top with another layer of salad, ricotta and tomato. Fold back the final layer of pasta and garnish with a little salad and tomato. Repeat with the remaining pasta, salad, ricotta and tomato to make four servings. Just before serving, drizzle with balsamic syrup and garnish with Parmesan.

NUTRITION PER SERVE
Protein 18 g; Fat 16 g; Carbohydrate 36 g;
Dietary Fibre 6 g; Cholesterol 63 mg;
1515 kJ (360 Cal)

Simmer the balsamic vinegar and brown sugar until it becomes syrupy.

Toss the peas, asparagus, zucchini, rocket, basil and olive oil together.

Fold one third of the lasagne sheet over the salad mix, ricotta and tomato.

SWEET CITRUS SCALLOP SALAD

Preparation time: 20 minutes
Total cooking time: 20 minutes
Serves 4

LEMON AND HERB DRESSING
1/2 preserved lemon
1/4 cup (60 ml/2 fl oz) olive oil
2 tablespoons lemon juice
1 tablespoon sweet chilli sauce
2 tablespoons white wine vinegar
2 tablespoons chopped
    coriander
500 g (1 lb) potatoes
oil, for shallow-frying

750 g (1 lb 10 oz) scallops, without
    roe
2 tablespoons olive oil, extra
75 g (2¹/2 oz) baby English spinach
    leaves

1 For the dressing, scoop out and discard the pulp from the preserved lemon, wash the skin and cut into thin slices. Put in a bowl and whisk with the olive oil, lemon juice, sweet chilli sauce, wine vinegar and coriander.
2 Cut the potatoes into paper-thin slices. Heat 2 cm (³/4 inch) oil in a deep heavy-based frying pan and cook batches of the potato for 1–2 minutes, or until crisp and golden. Drain on crumpled paper towels.

3 Slice or pull off any membrane, vein or hard white muscle from the scallops. Heat the extra oil in a frying pan over high heat and cook batches of scallops for 1–2 minutes, or until golden brown on both sides.
4 Divide half the spinach among four plates. Top with potato, then half the scallops and more spinach. Finish with more scallops. Drizzle with the dressing just before serving.

NUTRITION PER SERVE
Protein 25.5 g; Fat 30.5 g; Carbohydrate 20 g;
Dietary Fibre 3.5 g; Cholesterol 62 mg; 1890 kJ
(450 Cal)

Use a spoon to scoop out the pulpy centre from the preserved lemon.

Remove the crisp golden potato crisps from the oil with a slotted spoon.

Cook batches of scallops until golden on both sides.

CHICKEN SALAD WITH MUSTARD DRESSING

Preparation time: 30 minutes
Total cooking time: 15 minutes
Serves 6

150 g (5 oz) snow peas, trimmed
1 tablespoon oil
20 g (^{3}/4 oz) butter
4 chicken breast fillets
1 carrot, cut into julienne strips
2 celery sticks, cut into julienne strips
3 spring onions, cut into julienne strips
150 g (5 oz) button mushrooms, sliced
^{1}/3 cup (7 g/^{1}/4 oz) fresh flat-leaf parsley, chopped
1 tablespoon chopped fresh tarragon
150 g (5 oz) watercress or baby English spinach leaves
2 tablespoons almonds, chopped

DRESSING
^{1}/4 cup (60 ml/2 fl oz) extra virgin olive oil
1 tablespoon white wine vinegar
^{1}/2 teaspoon sugar
^{1}/4 cup (60 g/2 oz) mayonnaise
2 tablespoons sour cream
1 tablespoon Dijon mustard

1 Plunge the snow peas into a pan of boiling water, return to the boil and cook for 1 minute, or until tender but still crisp. Rinse under cold water and drain well. Cut diagonally into strips.
2 Heat the oil and butter in a frying pan, add the chicken and cook for 7 minutes on each side over medium heat, or until tender and well browned all over. Drain on paper towels and allow to cool. Cut into thin slices.
3 Mix together the carrot, celery, spring onion, snow peas, chicken, mushrooms, parsley and tarragon, and season with salt and black pepper.
4 To make the dressing, combine the oil, vinegar and sugar in a jug. Whisk until well blended, then season with salt and freshly ground black pepper. Add the mayonnaise, sour cream and mustard and whisk until well blended. Place the watercress in a serving dish, top with the chicken salad, drizzle with the dressing and sprinkle with the almonds.

NUTRITION PER SERVE
Protein 20 g; Fat 25 g; Carbohydrate 5 g;
Dietary Fibre 4 g; Cholesterol 60 mg;
1415 kJ (335 Cal)

VARIATION: Add a sliced avocado and use fresh asparagus instead of snow peas.

Using a small knife, trim the mushrooms and cut into thin slices.

Cook the chicken over medium heat until well browned and tender.

Add the mayonnaise, sour cream and mustard and whisk until well blended.

PRAWN NOODLE SALAD

Preparation time: 25 minutes
Total cooking time: 5 minutes
Serves 4

125 g (4 oz) snowpeas
750 g (1 lb 10 oz) medium raw
    prawns, peeled and deveined
375 g (12 oz) thin fresh egg
    noodles
150 g (5 oz) bean sprouts
4 spring onions, finely sliced
1 red capsicum, diced
5 tablespoons chopped
    coriander

DRESSING
1/4 cup (60 ml/2 fl oz) sesame oil
1/3 cup (80 ml/2³/4 fl oz) red wine
    vinegar
1/3 cup (80 ml/2³/4 fl oz) kecap manis
2 tablespoons soy sauce

1 Trim the snowpeas and cook them in a small saucepan of boiling water for 1 minute, then transfer to a bowl of iced water. When cold, drain and cut any large ones in half.
2 Cook the prawns in a large saucepan of boiling water for 1–2 minutes, or until the prawns turn pink and are cooked through. Drain and cool, but do not refrigerate.

3 Cook the noodles in a large saucepan of rapidly boiling salted water for 1 minute, or until tender. Drain and leave to cool.
4 For the dressing, thoroughly whisk the ingredients together in a small bowl or jug.
5 Put the snowpeas, prawns, noodles, bean sprouts, spring onion, capsicum and coriander in a large bowl. Add the dressing, toss gently and serve immediately.

NUTRITION PER SERVE
Protein 34.5 g; Fat 16 g; Carbohydrate
28 g; Dietary Fibre 3.5 g; Cholesterol 186.5 mg;
1660 kJ (395 Cal)

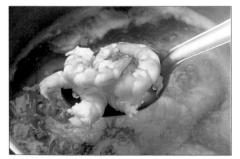
When the prawns are cooked, remove from the water with a slotted spoon.

Test the noodles after 1 minute to see if they are tender. Don't overcook.

Whisk the dressing ingredients together in a small bowl or jug.

WARM MINTED CHICKEN PASTA SALAD

Preparation time: 15 minutes
Total cooking time: 20 minutes
Serves 4

250 g (8 oz) pasta
1/2 cup (125 ml/4 fl oz) olive oil
1 large red capsicum
3 chicken breast fillets
6 spring onions, cut into short lengths
4 cloves garlic, thinly sliced
3/4 cup (35 g/1 1/4 oz) chopped fresh mint
1/3 cup (80 ml/2 3/4 fl oz) cider vinegar
100 g (3 1/2 oz) baby English spinach

1 Cook the pasta in a large pan of rapidly boiling salted water until *al dente*. Drain, return to the pan to keep warm and toss with a tablespoon of the oil.
2 Meanwhile, cut the capsicum into quarters, removing the seeds and membrane. Place, skin-side-up, under a hot grill (broiler) for 8–10 minutes, or until the skin blackens and blisters. Cool in a plastic bag, then peel away the skin. Cut into thin strips. Place the chicken between two sheets of plastic wrap and press with the palm of your hand until slightly flattened.
3 Heat 1 tablespoon of the oil in a large frying pan, add the chicken and cook over medium heat for 2–3 minutes each side, or until light brown and cooked through. Remove from the pan and cut into thin slices.

4 Add another tablespoon of the oil to the pan and add the spring onion, garlic and capsicum. Cook, stirring, for 2–3 minutes, or until starting to soften. Add most of the mint, the vinegar and the remaining oil and stir until warmed through. Toss together the pasta, chicken, spinach, onion mixture and remaining mint. Serve warm.

NUTRITION PER SERVE
Protein 47 g; Fat 30 g; Carbohydrate 47g;
Dietary Fibre 6 g; Cholesterol 84 mg;
2705 kJ (645 Cal)

Place the chicken between two sheets of plastic wrap and flatten slightly with your hand.

Brown the chicken until cooked through and then cut into slices.

PASTA AND BEAN SALAD WITH CUMIN AND CORIANDER DRESSING

Preparation time: 25 minutes
Total cooking time: 15 minutes
Serves 6

300 g (10 oz) spiral pasta
2 tablespoons sunflower oil
1 leek, sliced
1 red capsicum, seeded and diced
2 cups (125 g/4 oz) finely shredded
   English spinach
150 g (5 oz) button mushrooms,
   halved
300 g (10 oz) can red kidney beans,
   rinsed and drained
300 g (10 oz) can butter beans, rinsed
   and drained
2 tablespoons snipped chives
1/2 teaspoon coarsely ground black
   pepper
60 g (2 oz) sunflower seeds, toasted

CUMIN AND CORIANDER DRESSING
2 cloves garlic, crushed
1/2 teaspoon ground cumin
1/2 teaspoon ground coriander
2 tablespoons cider vinegar
1/2 cup (125 ml/4 fl oz) olive oil

1 Cook the pasta in a large pan of rapidly boiling salted water until *al dente*. Drain well.
2 Heat the oil in a large pan, add the leek and capsicum and stir-fry over medium heat for 2–3 minutes. Add the spinach and mushrooms and toss together for about 1 minute, or until the spinach just wilts.
3 To make the dressing, mix the garlic, cumin, coriander and vinegar together. Gradually add the olive oil and whisk to combine.

4 Toss together the pasta, vegetables, beans, chives and black pepper. Toss with the dressing and sprinkle with the sunflower seeds to serve.

NUTRITION PER SERVE
Protein 15 g; Fat 30 g; Carbohydrate 45 g;
Dietary Fibre 10 g; Cholesterol 0 mg;
2215 kJ (525 cal)

Add the spinach and mushrooms to the leek and capsicum and cook until the spinach wilts.

Gradually whisk the oil into the combined garlic, cumin, coriander and vinegar.

Pour the dressing into the salad and toss gently to mix through.

WARM ITALIAN SALAD

Preparation time: 15 minutes
Total cooking time: 15 minutes
Serves 4

olive oil, for cooking
4 slices prosciutto
2 onions, cut into wedges
1 clove garlic, crushed
250 g (8 oz) cherry tomatoes
1 yellow capsicum, cut into squares
1 green capsicum, cut into squares
180 g (6 oz) marinated artichoke
   hearts, halved

100 g (3¹/₂ oz) black olives
150 g (5 oz) rocket leaves
1 tablespoon balsamic vinegar
1 tablespoon extra virgin olive oil
Parmesan shavings, to serve

1 Heat the wok until very hot, add 2 teaspoons of the oil and swirl it around to coat the side. Stir-fry the prosciutto until crisp and golden. Drain on paper towels and crumble.
2 Reheat the wok, add 2 teaspoons of the oil and stir-fry the onion and garlic over high heat for 3–4 minutes, or until tender.
3 Stir in the tomatoes, capsicum and

artichokes, and cook for 4–5 minutes, or until tender. Add the olives and rocket and stir-fry until the rocket has just wilted.
4 Combine the vinegar and olive oil, and season. Pour into the wok and toss thoroughly. Serve immediately, sprinkled with the prosciutto and Parmesan shavings.

NUTRITION PER SERVE
Protein 7.5 g; Fat 20 g; Carbohydrate 5 g;
Dietary Fibre 3.5 g; Cholesterol 10 mg;
870 kJ (210 Cal)

Stir-fry the prosciutto slices until they are crisp and golden.

Drain the prosciutto on paper towels, then crumble into pieces with your fingers.

Stir the tomatoes, capsicum and artichokes into the onion and garlic.

TUNA AND OLIVE PASTA SALAD

Preparation time: 10 minutes
Total cooking time: 15 minutes
Serves 4–6

350 g (11 oz) spaghetti
8 quail eggs (or 4 hen eggs)
1 lemon
3 x 185 g (6 oz) cans tuna in oil
¹/₃ cup (60 g/2 oz) pitted and halved
     Kalamata olives
100 g (3¹/₂ oz) semi-dried tomatoes,
     halved lengthways
4 anchovy fillets, chopped into small
     pieces
3 tablespoons baby capers, drained
3 tablespoons chopped fresh flat-leaf
     parsley

1 Cook the pasta in a large pan of rapidly boiling salted water until *al dente*. Drain and return to the pan to keep warm. Meanwhile, place the eggs in a saucepan of cold water, bring to the boil and cook for 4 minutes (10 minutes for hen eggs). Drain, cool under cold water, then peel. Cut the quail eggs in half or the hen eggs into quarters. Finely grate the rind of the lemon to give 1 teaspoon of grated rind. Then, squeeze the lemon to give 2 tablespoons juice.

2 Empty the tuna and its oil into a large bowl. Add the olives, tomato halves, anchovies, lemon rind and juice, capers and 2 tablespoons of the parsley. Drain the pasta and rinse in a little cold water, then toss gently through the tuna mixture. Garnish with egg and the extra parsley.

NUTRITION PER SERVE (6)
Protein 32 g; Fat 26 g; Carbohydrate 47 g;
Dietary Fibre 5 g; Cholesterol 153 mg;
2300 kJ (550 Cal)

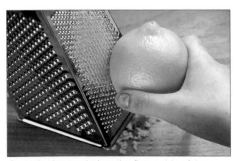
Grate the lemon rind on the finest side of the grater, avoiding the white pith beneath the rind.

Toss together the pasta and tuna mixture, then garnish with the egg and parsley.

84

CHICKEN AND SESAME NOODLE SALAD

Preparation time: 20 minutes +
  cooling time + 4 hours refrigeration
Cooking time: 15 minutes
Serves 4

1 chicken breast fillet (250 g/8 oz)
2 spring onions, chopped
3 cups (750 ml/24 fl oz) chicken stock
200 g (7 oz) mung bean vermicelli
2 Lebanese cucumbers, seeded and
  julienned into 5 cm (2 inch) lengths
2 spring onions, extra, sliced
2 tablespoons toasted sesame seeds

DRESSING
2 tablespoons Chinese sesame paste
2 tablespoons light soy sauce
1 tablespoon rice vinegar
1/4 teaspoon chilli oil
1 1/2 teaspoons sugar

1 Season the chicken breast well with salt and black pepper. Put the spring onion on the bottom of a wok and place the chicken breast on top. Gently pour in the stock, bring to a simmer over low heat and cook, covered, for 10 minutes, or until just cooked. Remove the chicken and set aside to cool, reserving the liquid.
2 Place the vermicelli in a heatproof bowl, cover with boiling water and soak for 3–4 minutes. Drain and rinse under cold water.
3 Meanwhile, to make the dressing, blend the sesame paste, soy sauce, rice vinegar, chilli oil, sugar and 150 ml (5 fl oz) of the reserved poaching liquid in a blender until smooth.
4 Shred the chicken meat. Toss in a bowl with the cucumber, noodles, extra spring onion and dressing until well combined. Cover with a plastic wrap and refrigerate for 4 hours.

5 To serve, sprinkle the salad with the toasted sesame seeds.

NUTRITION PER SERVE
Protein 19.5 g; Fat 13.5 g; Carbohydrate 30.5 g; Dietary Fibre 5 g; Cholesterol 41 mg; 1350 kJ (325 Cal)

NOTE: This recipe can be served as individual portions in lettuce cups.

Pour the sesame paste dressing over the salad ingredients.

SMOKED TUNA AND WHITE BEAN SALAD WITH BASIL DRESSING

Preparation time: 15 minutes
Total cooking time: Nil
Serves 4

100 g (3¹/2 oz) rocket
1 small red capsicum,
    cut in julienne strips
1 small red onion, chopped
310 g (10¹/2 oz) can cannellini
    beans or white beans, drained
    and rinsed
125 g (4 oz) cherry tomatoes,
    cut in halves

2 tablespoons capers
2 x 125 g (4 oz) cans smoked tuna
    slices in oil, drained

BASIL DRESSING
1 tablespoon lemon juice
1 tablespoon white wine
1/4 cup (60 ml/2 fl oz) extra virgin olive
    oil
1 clove garlic, crushed
2 teaspoons chopped basil
1/2 teaspoon sugar

1 Trim any long stems from the rocket, rinse, pat dry and divide among four serving plates.
2 Lightly toss the capsicum in a large bowl with the onion, beans, tomatoes and capers. Spoon some onto each plate, over the rocket, then scatter tuna over each.
3 For the dressing, thoroughly whisk all the ingredients in a bowl with 1 tablespoon of water, 1/4 teaspoon of salt and freshly ground or cracked black pepper, to taste. Drizzle over the salad and serve with bread.

NUTRITION PER SERVE
Protein 16 g; Fat 21 g; Carbohydrate 10 g;
Dietary Fibre 5.5 g; Cholesterol 18 mg;
1230 kJ (295 Cal)

ALTERNATIVE FISH: Fresh tuna, seared on both sides, then sliced, or canned salmon or tuna.

Cut the red capsicum lengthways into julienne strips.

Use two wooden spoons to toss the capsicum with the other ingredients.

Add the water, salt and pepper to the dressing ingredients and whisk well.

PACIFIC CHICKEN SALAD

Preparation time: 20 minutes
Total cooking time: 15 minutes
Serves 4

1 cup (250 ml/8 fl oz) coconut milk
1 tablespoon fish sauce
1 tablespoon grated palm sugar
4 chicken breast fillets
2 mangoes, thinly sliced
4 spring onions, sliced
1/4 cup (7 g/1/4 oz) fresh coriander
    leaves
1/3 cup (45 g/1 1/2 oz) coarsely
    chopped roasted unsalted
    macadamia nuts

DRESSING
2 tablespoons oil
1 teaspoon finely grated lime rind
2 tablespoons lime juice

1 Place the coconut milk, fish sauce and palm sugar in a frying pan and bring to the boil, stirring. Reduce the heat, add the chicken fillets and gently simmer, covered, for 10 minutes, or until the chicken is just tender. Leave to cool in the coconut liquid, then remove and pour the liquid into a jug.
2 To make the dressing, put 1/2 cup (125 ml/4 fl oz) of the reserved coconut cooking liquid, the oil, lime rind and juice in a small bowl and whisk to combine. Season to taste with salt and pepper.
3 Cut each chicken fillet diagonally into long slices and arrange on individual serving plates or in a large serving bowl. Spoon the dressing over the chicken and top with the sliced mango, spring onion, coriander leaves and macadamia nuts.

NUTRITION PER SERVE
Protein 30 g; Fat 35 g; Carbohydrate 15 g;
Dietary Fibre 2 g; Cholesterol 55 mg;
1965 kJ (465 cal)

NOTE: Palm sugar is obtained from either the palmyra palm or sugar palm, and is available in block form or in jars. It can be grated or gently melted before using. Soft brown sugar may be substituted.

Cut the mangoes into thin slices and carefully remove the skin.

Using a sharp knife, coarsely chop the macadamia nuts.

Put the coconut milk, fish sauce and palm sugar in a pan.

Cut each of the cooked chicken fillets into long diagonal slices.

SQUID AND SCALLOPS WITH HERB DRESSING

Preparation time: 30 minutes
+ 30 minutes chilling
Total cooking time: 10 minutes
Serves 4

2 oranges
8 baby squid
200 g (6 1/2 oz) scallops, without roe
2 tablespoons oil
150 g (5 oz) rocket
3 ripe Roma tomatoes, chopped

HERB DRESSING
1 cup (50 g/1 3/4 oz) finely chopped
coriander
1 cup (30 g/1 oz) finely chopped
flat-leaf parsley
2 teaspoons ground cumin
1 teaspoon paprika
1/4 cup (60 ml/2 fl oz) lime juice
1/4 cup (60 ml/2 fl oz) olive oil

1 Remove the skin and white pith from the oranges. Use a small sharp knife to cut between the membranes and divide into segments. Remove the seeds. Set aside.
2 To clean the squid, gently pull the tentacles away from the hoods (the intestines should come away at the same time). Remove the intestines from the tentacles by cutting under the eyes, then remove the beaks, if they remain in the centre of the tentacles, by using your finger to push up the centre. Pull away the soft bones (quill) from the hoods. Rub the hoods under cold running water and the skin should come away easily. Wash the hoods and tentacles and drain. Place in a bowl of water with 1/4 teaspoon salt and mix well. Cover and

refrigerate for about 30 minutes. Drain and cut the tubes into long thin strips and the tentacles into pieces.
3 Pull or slice off any membrane, vein or hard white muscle from the scallops. Rinse and pat dry.
4 Heat the oil in a large deep frying pan over high heat and cook the squid in batches for 1–2 minutes, or until it turns white. Do not overcook or it will be tough. Drain on paper towels. Add the scallops to the pan and cook for 1–2 minutes each side, or until tender.

Do not overcook.
5 Arrange the rocket on a large platter, top with seafood, tomatoes and orange segments.
6 Whisk the dressing ingredients together in a non-metallic bowl, then pour over the seafood.

NUTRITION PER SERVE
Protein 29 g; Fat 26 g; Carbohydrate 8 g;
Dietary Fibre 3.5 g; Cholesterol 265 mg;
1595 kJ (380 Cal)

Release the orange segments by cutting through with a small sharp knife.

Gently pull the tentacles and intestines away from the squid hoods.

If the beak remains, remove it by using your finger to push up the centre.

CHICKEN AND WATERCRESS SALAD

Preparation time: 40 minutes
Total cooking time: 10–15 minutes
Serves 4

3 small chicken breast fillets
    (350 g/11 oz)
1 Lebanese cucumber
1/2 red capsicum
150 g (5 oz) watercress
1/2 cup (10 g/1/4 oz) fresh mint leaves
2 tablespoons finely shredded fresh
    mint
2 chillies, thinly sliced
2 tablespoons crisp-fried onion

DRESSING
1/4 cup (60 ml/2 fl oz) lime juice
2 tablespoons coconut milk
1 tablespoon fish sauce
1 tablespoon sweet chilli sauce

1 Line a bamboo steamer with baking paper and steam the chicken, covered, over a wok or pan of simmering water, for 10 minutes or until the chicken is cooked through. Remove from the heat and set aside to cool. Thinly slice the cucumber and cut the slices in half. Slice the capsicum into thin strips.
2 While the chicken is cooling, pick over the watercress and separate the sprigs from the tough stems. Arrange the watercress and whole mint leaves on a serving plate. Using your fingers, tear the chicken into long, thin shreds. Gently toss the shredded chicken, cucumber and capsicum in a bowl. Arrange over the watercress bed.
3 To make the dressing, whisk the lime juice, coconut milk, fish sauce and sweet chilli sauce until combined.

4 Drizzle the dressing over the salad and sprinkle with the shredded mint, sliced chillies and crisp-fried onion.

NUTRITION PER SERVE
Protein 40 g; Fat 6 g; Carbohydrate 3 g;
Dietary Fibre 2.5 g; Cholesterol 82 mg;
966 kJ (230 cal)

NOTE: Crisp-fried, or sometimes deep-fried, onions are available in packets or small jars from Asian supermarkets.

Line a bamboo steamer with baking paper and cook the chicken.

Pick over the watercress to separate the sprigs from the tough stems.

When the chicken is cooked, tear it into shreds, using your fingers.

TUNA AND SOY BEAN SALAD WITH GINGER DRESSING

Preparation time: 35 minutes
Total cooking time: 10 minutes
Serves 4

GINGER DRESSING
1/4 cup (60 ml/2 fl oz) soy bean oil
2 tablespoons white wine vinegar
1 tablespoon grated fresh ginger
2 teaspoons honey
2 teaspoons salt-reduced soy
    sauce

2 carrots, sliced on the diagonal
2 zucchini, sliced on the diagonal
1 red capsicum, cut into 2 cm
    (3/4 inch) cubes
4 tuna steaks (about 180 g/6 oz
    each), cubed
soy bean oil, for brushing
1/2 small red onion, cut into thin
    wedges
150 g (5 oz) cherry tomatoes, halved
300 g (10 oz) can soy beans, rinsed
    and drained
1 tablespoon baby capers
125 g (4 oz) baby rocket leaves

1 To make the ginger dressing, place the oil, vinegar, ginger, honey and soy sauce in a jar and shake well.
2 Bring a saucepan of water to the boil. Add the carrot, zucchini and capsicum and cook, covered, for 1 minute. Drain and cool quickly under cold running water. Drain well.
3 Pat the tuna cubes dry with paper towels, then brush lightly with a little oil. Cook on a hot chargrill or barbecue plate for 1–2 minutes each side, or until cooked to your liking—the centre should still be pink.

4 Place the blanched vegetables, onion, tomato, soy beans, capers and rocket in a large bowl. Add the dressing and toss together. Divide among four serving bowls and toss in the cubes of tuna. Serve immediately.

NUTRITION PER SERVE
Protein 35 g; Fat 30 g; Carbohydrate 10 g;
Dietary Fibre 7 g; Cholesterol 50 mg;
1359 kJ (325 Cal)

Rinse the canned beans with cold water and drain well.

Vigorously shake the ginger dressing ingredients in a jar to combine.

Chargrill the cubes of tuna until cooked to your liking.

SICHUAN CHICKEN AND NOODLE SALAD

Preparation time: 15 minutes +
   cooling time
Cooking time: 15 minutes
Serves 4

5 cm x 5 cm (2 inch x 2 inch) piece
   ginger, sliced
1/2 teaspoon black peppercorns
2 tablespoons celery leaves
8 spring onions, thinly sliced
3 chicken breast fillets (about 200 g/
   6 1/2 oz each)
1 teaspoon Sichuan peppercorns
500 g (1 lb) dried somen noodles
3 tablespoons crisp fried garlic flakes
40 g (1 1/2 oz) shredded Chinese
   broccoli (gai lan) leaves
2 small Lebanese cucumbers, cut
   into batons

DRESSING
1/2 teaspoon sesame oil
1/3 cup (80 ml/2 3/4 fl oz) light soy
   sauce
1 tablespoon Chinese black vinegar
2 teaspoons Chinese rice wine

1 Place the ginger, peppercorns, celery leaves, half the spring onion, 1 teaspoon salt and the chicken in a large saucepan. Add enough cold water to cover and bring to the boil over high heat. Reduce the heat to medium, cover and simmer for 10 minutes, or until cooked through. Remove the chicken, cool slightly and cut into 1.5 cm (5/8 inch) slices on the diagonal.
2 Meanwhile, dry-fry the Sichuan peppercorns in a frying pan for 1 minute, or until the peppercorns are dark and aromatic. Place in a spice grinder or mortar and pestle and grind to a fine powder.
3 To make the dressing, whisk the sesame oil, light soy sauce, black vinegar and Chinese rice wine until well combined.
4 Cook the noodles in a large saucepan of boiling water for 2 minutes, or until tender. Drain and rinse under cold water, then drain again. Transfer to a large bowl and add the chicken, crisp fried garlic flakes,

Chinese broccoli leaves, cucumber, ground Sichuan pepper, the dressing and the remaining spring onion and toss until well combined. Season to taste with salt and freshly ground black pepper and serve.

NUTRITION PER SERVE
Protein 39 g; Fat 9.5 g; Carbohydrate 33.5 g; Dietary Fibre 3.5 g; Cholesterol 99 mg; 1595 kJ (380 Cal)

Dry-fry the peppercorns in a clean frying pan until they darken.

WARM SWEET POTATO, WALNUT AND PASTA SALAD

Preparation time: 15 minutes
Total cooking time: 30 minutes
Serves 4

800 g (1 lb 10 oz) orange sweet
   potato, cut into small cubes
150 ml (5 fl oz) olive oil
1 cup (125 g/4 oz) walnut pieces
350 g (11 oz) pasta
150 g (5 oz) white castello cheese
2 cloves garlic, crushed
2 teaspoons lemon juice
1/2 teaspoon sugar
100 g (3¹/₂ oz) rocket

1 Preheat the oven to moderately hot 200°C (400°F/Gas 6). Toss the orange sweet potato in 2 tablespoons of the oil and place in a single layer on a baking tray lined with baking paper. Season with salt and pepper. Cook, turning halfway through, for 30 minutes, or until golden and cooked through. Spread the walnuts onto a separate baking tray and add to the oven for the last 10 minutes, or until crisp and golden.
2 Meanwhile, cook the pasta in a large pan of rapidly boiling salted water until *al dente*. Drain well and return to the pan to keep warm. Remove the rind from one-third of the cheese and cut the rest into cubes. Finely chop 2 tablespoons of the

toasted walnuts and place in a jar with the garlic, lemon juice, sugar, remaining oil and rindless cheese and season. Shake the jar until well combined. You may need to break the cheese up with a fork to help mix it through if it is too firm.
3 Toss the pasta, sweet potato, rocket, cubed cheese and remaining walnuts in a bowl, drizzle with the dressing and toss together. Divide among four serving bowls and season to taste with salt and black pepper.

NUTRITION PER SERVE
Protein 27 g; Fat 69 g; Carbohydrate 92 g;
Dietary Fibre 11 g; Cholesterol 38 mg;
4570 kJ (1090 cal)

Spread the walnuts on a baking tray and toast for 10 minutes.

Remove the rind from one-third of the cheese and cut the rest into cubes.

Toss together the pasta, sweet potato, rocket, cheese and walnuts.

SALMON, LEEK AND CAMEMBERT SALAD

Preparation time: 10 minutes
Total cooking time: 15 minutes
Serves 4

500 g (1 lb) salmon fillet, cut into thick
   strips
1/4 cup (60 g/2 oz) wholegrain
   mustard
1 tablespoon lime juice
2 tablespoons oil
1 leek, white part only, julienned
2 tablespoons tamari
2 teaspoons fish sauce

1 tablespoon honey
75 g (2^1/$_2$ oz) snow pea sprouts
1/2 cup (15 g/^{1}/$_2$ oz) coriander leaves,
   plus extra to garnish
100 g (3^1/$_2$ oz) Camembert, sliced
lime wedges, to serve

1 Place the salmon strips in a glass
or ceramic bowl. Add the mustard and
lime juice and toss to coat the salmon.
2 Heat the wok until very hot, add the
oil and swirl it around to coat the side.
Stir-fry the salmon in batches over
high heat until it is slightly browned.
Remove from the wok.
3 Add 1 tablespoon water to the wok,
then add the leek and stir-fry until it

is golden brown. Return the salmon
to the wok, with the tamari, fish sauce
and honey. Cook until the salmon is
heated through.
4 Remove the wok from the heat
and toss the snow pea sprouts and
coriander leaves through the salmon.
Serve topped with the Camembert and
extra coriander, and the lime wedges
on the side.

NUTRITION PER SERVE
Protein 30 g; Fat 30 g; Carbohydrate 7 g;
Dietary Fibre 2 g; Cholesterol 110 mg;
1770 kJ (420 Cal)

Remove the skin from the salmon, pull out any
bones, then cut into thick strips.

Cut the leek into julienne strips, using only the
white part.

Stir-fry the salmon until it turns a soft pink colour
and is slightly browned.

SALAMI PASTA SALAD

Preparation time: 20 minutes
Total cooking time: 15 minutes
Serves 8

1 red capsicum, cut into strips
1 green capsicum, cut into strips
4 celery stalks, sliced
1 fennel bulb, trimmed and sliced
1 red onion, sliced
200 g (6¹/₂ oz) salami, thickly sliced
    and then cut into strips

¹/₂ cup (15 g/¹/₂ oz) chopped fresh
    flat-leaf parsley
300 g (10 oz) fettucine

DRESSING
¹/₂ cup (125 ml/4 fl oz) olive oil
3 tablespoons lemon juice
2¹/₂ tablespoons Dijon mustard
1 teaspoon sugar
1 clove garlic, crushed

1 Mix together the red and green capsicum, celery, fennel, onion, salami and parsley in a large bowl.

2 Cook the pasta in a large pan of rapidly boiling salted water until *al dente*. Drain well and rinse under cold water. Add to the bowl and toss with the vegetables and salami.
3 To make the dressing, combine the olive oil, lemon juice, mustard, sugar and crushed garlic and season to taste. Pour over the salad and toss well.

NUTRITION PER SERVE
Protein 10 g; Fat 25 g; Carbohydrate 30 g;
Dietary Fibre 2.5 g; Cholesterol 26 mg;
1599 kJ (380 cal)

Use a sharp knife to halve the fennel and then cut into slices.

Cut the salami into strips and add to the bowl along with the chopped parsley.

To make the dressing, put the ingredients in a bowl and whisk together with a fork.

CHICKEN SALAD WITH ROCKET AND CANNELLINI BEANS

Preparation time: 10 minutes
Total cooking time: 10 minutes
Serves 4

1/3 cup (80 ml/2¾ fl oz) lemon juice
3 cloves garlic, crushed
1 teaspoon soft brown sugar

1/4 cup (15 g/½ oz) fresh basil, finely
    chopped
1/2 cup (125 ml/4 fl oz) olive oil
4 chicken breast fillets
400 g (13 oz) can cannellini beans,
    rinsed and drained
100 g (3½ oz) small rocket leaves

1 Whisk together the lemon juice,
garlic, sugar, basil and olive oil.
2 Pour a third of the dressing over the
chicken to coat. Cook the chicken on a
hot, lightly oiled barbecue grill or
flatplate for 4 minutes on each side, or
until cooked through.
3 Meanwhile, combine the beans and
rocket with the remaining dressing,
toss well and season. Slice the chicken
and serve over the rocket and beans.

NUTRITION PER SERVE
Protein 35 g; Fat 35 g; Carbohydrate 13 g;
Dietary Fibre 7.5 g; Cholesterol 60 mg;
2045 kJ (490 cal)

Whisk together the lemon juice, garlic, sugar, basil and olive oil.

Cook the chicken on a hot grill or flatplate until cooked through.

Slice the chicken and serve on top of the rocket and cannellini beans.

SESAME TUNA AND EGG NOODLE SALAD

Preparation time: 20 minutes
Cooking time: 5 minutes
Serves 4

300 g (10¹/2 oz) fresh flat egg noodles
100 g (3¹/2 oz) watercress, trimmed
2 small Lebanese cucumbers, halved
    lengthways, thinly sliced
1 small red capsicum, seeded and
    thinly sliced
¹/3 cup (10 g/¹/4 oz) coriander leaves
¹/4 cup (40 g/1¹/4 oz) sesame seeds
¹/4 cup (40 g/1¹/4 oz) black sesame
    seeds
3 tuna steaks (about 550 g/1 lb 4 oz)
peanut oil, to shallow-fry

DRESSING
¹/4 cup (60 ml/2 fl oz) kecap manis
1¹/2 tablespoons Chinese rice wine

1 Cook the noodles in a large saucepan of boiling water for 1 minute, or until tender. Drain and rinse under cold water, then drain again. Place in a large bowl with the watercress, cucumber, capsicum and coriander and toss together well.
2 To make the dressing, combine the kecap manis and Chinese rice wine in a small bowl. Pour over the noodle mixture and toss together until well combined.
3 Mix the sesame seeds together on a sheet of baking paper. Pat the tuna steaks dry with paper towel, then coat in the sesame seeds.
4 Fill a large frying pan to 1.5 cm (5/8 inch) with peanut oil and heat to 180°C (350°F), or until a cube of bread dropped into the oil browns in 15 seconds. Fry the tuna steaks for 1–2 minutes on each side—they should still be pink in the centre. Drain on paper towels, then cut into 1.5 cm

(5/8 inch) thick slices across the grain using a very sharp knife.
5 To serve, divide the noodle salad among four serving bowls and arrange strips of tuna on top. Season with salt and freshly ground black pepper and serve immediately.

NUTRITION PER SERVE
Protein 47.5 g; Fat 24.5 g; Carbohydrate 41.5 g; Dietary Fibre 5 g; Cholesterol 59 mg; 2460 kJ (590 Cal)

NOTE: Slice the tuna immediately after cooking or it will continue to cook through and won't be rare in the centre.

PRAWN AND MANGO NOODLE SALAD

Preparation time: 25 minutes +
  5 minutes soaking + chilling time
Cooking time: Nil
Serves 4–6

DRESSING
1¹/₂ tablespoons fish sauce
2 tablespoons lime juice
2 teaspoons soft brown sugar
1 tablespoon sweet chilli sauce
2 teaspoons light soy sauce
1 small red chilli, seeded and finely
  sliced

150 g (5 oz) mung bean vermicelli
2 teaspoons peanut oil
1 large ripe mango (470 g/1 lb)
700 g (1 lb 9 oz) cooked medium
  prawns, peeled and deveined,
  well chilled

¹/₂ red onion, thinly sliced
¹/₂ cup (25 g/³/₄ oz) chopped
  coriander leaves
¹/₃ cup (20 g/³/₄ oz) chopped
  Vietnamese mint
50 g (1³/₄ oz) mizuna
2 tablespoons chopped roasted
  peanuts

1 To make the dressing, combine the fish sauce, lime juice, brown sugar, sweet chilli sauce, soy sauce and chilli in a small bowl and stir until the sugar has dissolved.
2 Place the noodles in a large heatproof bowl, cover with boiling water and soak for 3–4 minutes, or until softened. Drain and rinse under cold water. Cut into 10 cm (4 inch) lengths with scissors. Transfer to a large bowl, add the peanut oil and toss together well.
3 Peel the mango and cut into thin strips, about 3 mm (¹/₈ inch) wide.

Add to the noodles with the prawns, red onion, coriander leaves and mint. Pour the dressing on the salad and toss gently, taking care not to break up the mango slices or noodles.
4 To serve, arrange the mizuna on a large serving plate, spoon the salad on top and garnish with the chopped peanuts. Serve chilled.

NUTRITION PER SERVE (6)
Protein 26.5 g; Fat 4.5 g; Carbohydrate 20.5 g;
Dietary Fibre 2.5 g; Cholesterol 174 mg;
956 kJ (230 Cal)

HINT: Wear rubber gloves when working with chillies. And remember, the smaller the chilli the more intense the heat.

LAMB CUTLETS WITH BEETROOT, BEAN AND POTATO SALAD

Preparation time: 15 minutes +
overnight refrigeration
Total cooking time: 45 minutes
Serves 4

2 cloves garlic, crushed
2 tablespoons finely chopped
fresh thyme
1½ tablespoons lemon juice
1 tablespoon walnut oil
2 tablespoons extra virgin olive oil
12 lamb cutlets, trimmed
6 baby beetroots, trimmed
500 g (1 lb) kipfler potatoes, unpeeled
250 g (8 oz) baby green beans
2 tablespoons olive oil

DRESSING
1 clove garlic, crushed
3½ tablespoons lemon juice
⅓ cup (80 ml/2¾ fl oz) extra virgin
olive oil
1 tablespoon walnut oil
¼ cup (30 g/1 oz) chopped walnuts

1 Combine the garlic, thyme, lemon juice, walnut oil and extra virgin olive oil in a shallow, non-metallic dish, add the cutlets and toss well. Cover with plastic wrap and refrigerate overnight.
2 Cook the beetroots in boiling water for 20 minutes, or until tender. Drain. Meanwhile, cook the potatoes in lightly salted boiling water for 12 minutes, or until tender. Drain.
3 When cool enough to handle, peel the beetroots and potatoes. Cut each beetroot into six wedges and thickly slice the potatoes.
4 Cook the beans in lightly salted boiling water for 4 minutes. Drain, refresh under cold water, then drain

again. Pat dry with paper towels.
5 Heat the olive oil in a large frying pan over high heat and cook the cutlets in batches for 4–5 minutes, or until cooked to your liking, turning once.
6 Whisk the garlic, lemon juice, extra virgin olive oil and walnut oil in a large bowl. Add the potatoes, beans and walnuts and toss gently. Season and arrange over the beetroot. Top with the cutlets and serve.

NUTRITION PER SERVE
Protein 30 g; Fat 55 g; Carbohydrate 25 g;
Dietary Fibre 6.5 g; Cholesterol 70 mg;
2990 kJ (714 Cal)

Peel the beetroots and cut each one into six wedges.

Cook the cutlets in batches until done to your liking.

CHICKEN AND ASPARAGUS PASTA SALAD

Preparation time: 30 minutes
Total cooking time: 25 minutes
Serves 4

250 g (8 oz) chicken breast fillet
1¹/₂ cups (375 ml/12 fl oz) chicken
    stock
350 g (11 oz) spiral pasta
150 g (5 oz) asparagus, cut into short
    lengths
150 g (5 oz) Gruyère cheese, grated
2 spring onions, finely sliced

DRESSING
¹/₄ cup (60 ml/2 fl oz) olive oil
¹/₄ cup (60 ml/2 fl oz) lemon juice
¹/₂ teaspoon sugar

1 Put the chicken and stock in a frying pan. Bring to the boil, reduce the heat and poach gently, turning regularly, for 8 minutes, or until tender. Remove, cool and slice thinly.
2 Cook the pasta in a large pan of rapidly boiling salted water until *al dente*. Drain well and cool.
3 Cook the asparagus in boiling water for 2 minutes. Drain and place in a bowl of iced water. Drain again. Combine with the chicken, pasta and cheese in a large bowl.
4 To make the dressing, whisk the ingredients together. Season with salt and pepper. Add to the salad and toss well. Transfer to a serving bowl and scatter with the spring onions.

NUTRITION PER SERVE
Protein 40 g; Fat 30 g; Carbohydrate 60 g;
Dietary Fibre 5 g; Cholesterol 70 mg;
2785 kJ (665 Cal)

Grate the cheese, chop the asparagus and finely slice the spring onion.

Pour the stock over the chicken and poach over low heat, turning regularly.

Cook the asparagus in a small pan of boiling water for 2 minutes.

99

BEEF AND GLASS NOODLE SALAD

Preparation time: 25 minutes +
    5 minutes soaking
Cooking time: 10 minutes
Serves 4

500 g (1 lb) beef fillet, 5 cm
    (2 inch) in diameter
1¹/₂ tablespoons vegetable oil
1 teaspoon dried shrimp
1 teaspoon jasmine rice
1 stem lemon grass (white part only),
    finely chopped
1 small red chilli, seeded and
    finely chopped
2 coriander roots, finely chopped
2 kaffir lime leaves, finely shredded
1–2 tablespoons lime juice
2 teaspoons finely chopped
    ginger
300 g (10 oz) mung bean vermicelli
1 small Lebanese cucumber,
    peeled, cut in half lengthways
    and cut into 1 cm (¹/₂ inch)
    pieces
1 vine-ripened tomato, cut into 1 cm
    (¹/₂ inch) wedges
1 red onion, cut into thin wedges
3 tablespoons Thai basil, torn
3 tablespoons Vietnamese mint
1 tablespoon crisp fried shallots
2 tablespoons coriander leaves

DRESSING
¹/₃ cup (80 ml/2³/₄ fl oz) lime juice
2 tablespoons grated palm sugar
1 tablespoon fish sauce
1 small red chilli, seeded and
    finely chopped
1 teaspoon sesame oil
¹/₂ teaspoon tamarind purée

1 Heat a chargrill plate or frying pan over high heat. Brush the beef with the oil and season generously with salt and black pepper. Sear on all sides for 3–4 minutes ensuring the meat remains rare in the centre. Remove and allow to rest.
2 Meanwhile, dry-fry the dried shrimp and rice in a clean frying pan for 1–2 minutes, or until fragrant. Place in a spice grinder or mortar and pestle and grind to a fine powder. Mix the powder with the lemon grass, chilli, coriander roots, lime leaves, lime juice and ginger in a non-metallic bowl. Add the beef and turn to coat well on all sides. Cover and marinate for 5 minutes. Cut into 1 cm (¹/₂ inch) thick slices across the grain.
3 To make the dressing, combine all the ingredients in a small bowl.
4 Place the vermicelli in a heatproof bowl, cover with boiling water and soak for 3–4 minutes, or until softened. Drain, rinse under cold water and drain again. Transfer the noodles to a large bowl, then add the beef, cucumber, tomato, red onion, basil, mint and dressing and toss well. Serve garnished with the crisp fried shallots and coriander leaves.

NUTRITION PER SERVE
Protein 28.5g; Fat 12 g; Carbohydrate 48.5 g;
Dietary Fibre 4 g; Cholesterol 84 mg;
1765 kJ (420 Cal)

Add the beef to the marinade, then turn to coat well on all sides.

CHICKEN CITRUS SALAD WITH CURRY DRESSING

Preparation time: 20 minutes
Total cooking time: 15 minutes
Serves 4

4 chicken breast fillets
1 tablespoon olive oil
2 oranges
1 lettuce
250 g (8 oz) watercress
15 g (1/2 oz) fresh chives

CURRY DRESSING
3 teaspoons curry powder
2 spring onions, thinly sliced
2 tablespoons olive oil
2 tablespoons sunflower oil
1 tablespoon balsamic vinegar
2 teaspoons soft brown sugar
1 teaspoon chopped green chilli

1 Trim the chicken fillets of any fat and sinew. Heat the oil in a frying pan and cook the chicken over medium heat for about 7 minutes on each side, or until browned and tender. Allow to cool, then cut across the grain into thick strips.
2 To make the curry dressing, dry-fry the curry powder in a frying pan for 1 minute, or until fragrant. Cool slightly, then place in a small bowl with the spring onion, olive oil, sunflower oil, vinegar, sugar and chilli and whisk to combine. Season to taste with salt and black pepper. Set aside to allow the flavours to develop.
3 Peel the oranges, removing all the white pith. Cut into segments, between the membrane, and discard any pips.
4 Wash and dry the lettuce leaves and watercress and arrange on a large platter. Place the chicken pieces and orange segments on top. Whisk the dressing again, then drizzle it over the salad. Cut the chives into short lengths and scatter over the top.

NUTRITION PER SERVE
Protein 25 g; Fat 25 g; Carbohydrate 10 g;
Dietary Fibre 2 g; Cholesterol 55 mg;
1590 kJ (380 Cal)

Cook the chicken fillets until tender and browned on both sides.

Fry the curry powder in a dry frying pan for 1 minute, or until fragrant.

Carefully cut the oranges into segments between the membrane.

Whisk the curry dressing well before drizzling over the salad.

GREEK PASTA SALAD

Preparation time: 10 minutes
Total cooking time: 45 minutes
Serves 4

4 Roma tomatoes, quartered
1 tablespoon chopped fresh oregano
500 g (1 lb) rigatoni
250 g (8 oz) marinated soft feta
1 red onion, sliced
1 tablespoon capers in salt, rinsed
     and patted dry (see NOTE)
2 tablespoons red wine vinegar
1/2 cup (15 g/1/2 oz) chopped fresh
     flat-leaf parsley
2 tablespoons ready-made olive
     tapenade

1 Preheat the oven to moderate 180°C (350°F/Gas 4). Place the tomatoes cut-side-up on a baking tray, sprinkle with 1 teaspoon of the oregano and season well. Roast for 30–40 minutes, or until soft and caramelised.
2 Cook the pasta in a large pan of rapidly boiling salted water until *al dente*. Drain well and return to the pan to keep warm.
3 Drain and crumble the feta, reserving the oil and herbs. Heat 2 teaspoons of the reserved oil in a small frying pan, add the onion and cook over medium heat for 2–3 minutes, or until soft, then add the capers and cook for a further minute. Combine the rest of the reserved oil with the vinegar and stir into the pan.

Remove from the heat and stir through the pasta, adding the remaining oregano and the parsley. Top with the tomato, feta and the tapenade to serve.

NUTRITION PER SERVE
Protein 27 g; Fat 16 g; Carbohydrate 89 g;
Dietary Fibre 6 g; Cholesterol 43 mg;
2570 kJ (615 cal)

NOTE: You can buy capers in salt from delicatessens—they are smaller than normal capers and are kept in salt rather than brine. If you want to use capers in brine, buy baby capers and drain them before use.

Put the tomatoes cut-side-up on a baking tray and roast until soft.

Cook the pasta in rapidly boiling water until it is just tender.

Cook the onion until soft, then add the capers, oil and vinegar.

WARM PESTO AND PRAWN SALAD

Preparation time: 15 minutes
Total cooking time: 20 minutes
Serves 4

PESTO
2 cloves garlic, crushed
1 teaspoon salt
1/4 cup (40 g/1 1/4 oz) pine nuts, toasted
2 cups (60 g/2 oz) fresh basil
1/2 cup (60 g/2 oz) grated Parmesan
1/4 cup (60 ml/2 fl oz) extra virgin olive oil

500 g (1 lb) pasta
150 g (5 oz) jar capers in brine
3 tablespoons olive oil
2 tablespoons extra virgin olive oil
2 cloves garlic, chopped
2 tomatoes, seeded and diced
150 g (5 oz) thin asparagus, trimmed, halved and blanched
2 tablespoons balsamic vinegar
150 g (5 oz) rocket
20 cooked prawns, peeled, tails intact
shaved Parmesan, to garnish

1 For the pesto, blend the garlic, salt, pine nuts, fresh basil leaves and grated Parmesan in a food processor or blender until thoroughly combined. With the motor running, add the oil in a thin steady stream and process until the pesto is smooth.
2 Cook the pasta in a large pan of rapidly boiling salted water until *al dente*. Drain well, transfer to a large bowl and toss the pesto through.
3 Pat the drained capers dry with paper towels, then heat the olive oil in a frying pan and fry the capers for 4–5 minutes, stirring occasionally, until crisp. Drain on paper towels.
4 Heat the extra virgin olive oil in a deep frying pan over medium heat and add the garlic, tomatoes and asparagus. Toss continuously for 1–2 minutes, or until warmed through. Stir in the balsamic vinegar.
5 When the pasta is just warm, not hot (or it will wilt the rocket), toss the tomato mixture, rocket and prawns with the pasta and season with salt and pepper, to taste. Serve sprinkled with capers and shaved Parmesan.

NUTRITION PER SERVE
Protein 42 g; Fat 52 g; Carbohydrate 92 g; Dietary Fibre 10 g; Cholesterol 163 mg; 4195 kJ (1000 cal)

Use two wooden spoons to toss the pesto through the drained pasta.

Fry the drained capers in the hot oil, stirring occasionally, until crisp.

SOBA, SALMON AND AVOCADO SALAD

Preparation time: 25 minutes
Cooking time: 20 minutes
Serves 4

500 g (1 lb) salmon fillet, skin removed
1 tablespoon oil
1 avocado, halved and stone removed
500 g (1 lb) dried soba noodles
3 tablespoons pickled ginger, well
    drained and shredded
80 g (2³/₄ oz) mizuna, trimmed
¹/₃ cup (80 ml/2³/₄ fl oz) prepared
    ponzu sauce or ¹/₄ cup (60 ml/
    2 fl oz) soy sauce combined with
    1 tablespoon lemon juice
1 tablespoon black sesame seeds

1 Place the salmon in a bowl and rub the surface with the oil, salt and pepper. Slice each avocado half lengthways into quarters, then cut each quarter into 1 cm (¹/₂ inch) long pieces from the base to the stem end.
2 Heat a large frying pan over medium–high heat, and just before the pan begins to smoke add the salmon—if your fillet is too large to fit, cut it in half. Cook for 3 minutes on each side, or until golden—this will depend on the size and thickness of your fillet. Remove from the pan and allow to cool.
3 Bring a large saucepan of water to the boil over high heat. Add the noodles and stir to separate. Return to the boil, then add 1 cup (250 ml/ 8 fl oz) cold water. Repeat this step 3 times as the water just comes to the boil. Test a piece of soba—it should be tender to the bite, cooked through but not mushy. If it's not quite done, repeat one more time. Drain and rinse under cold water until the noodles are cold.
4 Combine the noodles, avocado, ginger and mizuna in a large bowl. Flake the salmon into small pieces with a fork or your fingers and add to the noodles with any juices, then add the ponzu sauce. Gently toss until well combined.
5 To serve, divide the noodle salad among the serving dishes and sprinkle with the sesame seeds.

NUTRITION PER SERVE
Protein 46 g; Fat 29.5 g; Carbohydrate 95.5 g; Dietary Fibre 4 g; Cholesterol 65 mg; 3345 kJ (800 Cal)

Use a fork to flake the salmon fillet into small pieces.

CHILLI SALT CHICKEN SALAD

Preparation time: 35 minutes
Total cooking time: 20 minutes
Serves 4

1 red capsicum, cut into julienne strips
  (see Note)
1 yellow capsicum, cut into julienne
  strips
4 spring onions, cut into julienne strips
1 cup (20 g/¾ oz) fresh mint leaves
1 cup (30 g/1 oz) fresh coriander
  leaves
3 chicken breast fillets
½ cup (60 g/2 oz) plain flour
1 tablespoon chilli powder
1 tablespoon onion powder
1 tablespoon garlic powder
1 tablespoon finely crushed
  sea salt
oil, for deep-frying

DRESSING
1 tablespoon sugar
2 tablespoons lemon juice
¼ cup (60 ml/2 fl oz) rice vinegar
¼ cup (60 ml/2 fl oz) peanut oil

1 Put the capsicum and spring onion strips in a bowl with the mint and coriander leaves.
2 To make the dressing, put the sugar, lemon juice, vinegar and oil in a bowl and whisk to combine.
3 Cut the chicken fillets into thin strips. Combine the flour, chilli powder, onion powder, garlic powder and salt in a plastic bag or shallow bowl. Add the chicken in batches and toss to coat in the flour mixture. Remove the chicken and shake off any excess flour.
4 Half fill a large heavy-based pan

with the oil. When the oil is hot, add the chicken in batches and deep-fry until it is golden brown. Drain well on paper towels. Add the chicken to the bowl with the vegetables and herbs, drizzle with the dressing and toss gently to combine. Serve immediately.

NUTRITION PER SERVE
Protein 20 g; Fat 30 g; Carbohydrate 20 g; Dietary Fibre 2 g; Cholesterol 40 mg; 1720 kJ (410 cal)

NOTE: Julienne strips are even-sized strips of vegetables, the size and shape of matchsticks.

Cut the capsicums and spring onions into julienne strips.

Remove the fat from the chicken and cut the fillets into long, thin strips.

Add the chicken strips to the spiced flour and toss to coat.

LAYERED SEAFOOD SALAD

Preparation time: 45 minutes
Total cooking time: 15 minutes
Serves 6

1 kg (2 lb) black mussels
24 scallops, with roe
1/2 cup (125 ml/4 fl oz) white wine
500 g (1 lb) skinless salmon or
    trout fillets
24 cooked king prawns, peeled
    and deveined
150 g (5 oz) mixed lettuce leaves
1 Lebanese cucumber, sliced

VINAIGRETTE
1/4 cup (60 ml/2 fl oz) light olive oil
1 tablespoon white wine vinegar
1 tablespoon lemon juice
1–2 teaspoons sugar
1 teaspoon Dijon mustard

CREAMY HERB DRESSING
2 egg yolks
2 teaspoons Dijon mustard
2 tablespoons lemon juice
1 cup (250 ml/8 fl oz) olive oil
4 anchovy fillets, chopped
1 clove garlic, crushed
1/4 cup (60 g/2 oz) sour cream
3 tablespoons chopped mixed herbs
    (e.g. parsley, dill)

1 Scrub the mussels with a stiff brush and pull out the beards. Discard any broken mussels, or open ones that don't close when tapped. Rinse well. Pull or slice off any vein, membrane or hard white muscle from the scallops. Put 1 cup (250 ml/8 fl oz) water in a large saucepan, add the wine and bring to the boil. Add the mussels, cover and steam for 4–5 minutes or until open. Remove with a slotted spoon. Discard any unopened ones. Remove the meat from the shells.
2 Add the scallops to the liquid and poach for 1–2 minutes, or until they just turn white, then remove. Add the fish to the liquid and poach for 4–5 minutes, or until just cooked. Remove and break into large pieces.
3 For the vinaigrette, put the ingredients in a screw top jar, season, tighten the lid and shake. Place all the seafood in a large bowl, add the vinaigrette and toss gently to coat.
4 For the creamy herb dressing, process the egg yolks, mustard and lemon juice in a food processor or blender for 30 seconds, or until light and creamy. With the motor running add the oil in a thin stream and process until thickened. Add the remaining ingredients and pulse for 30 seconds, or until combined.
5 Place half the lettuce and cucumber in a 2.25 litre (72 fl oz) glass serving bowl. Arrange half the seafood over the greens, then drizzle with half the dressing. Repeat with another layer of greens, seafood and dressing. Serve immediately with crusty bread.

NUTRITION PER SERVE
Protein 55.5 g; Fat 62 g; Carbohydrate 6.5 g;
Dietary Fibre 1 g; Cholesterol 282.5 mg;
3425 kJ (820 Cal)

ALTERNATIVE FISH: Swordfish, deep-sea perch.

Pull the shells apart and remove the mussel meat. Discard unopened mussels.

Layer the lettuce and cucumber, seafood and dressing in a serving bowl.

MEDITERRANEAN PASTA SALAD WITH BLACK OLIVE DRESSING

Preparation time: 30 minutes
Total cooking time: 25 minutes
Serves 4

250 g (8 oz) spiral pasta
1 red capsicum
1 yellow or green capsicum
1 tablespoon sunflower oil
2 tablespoons olive oil
2 cloves garlic, crushed
1 eggplant, cubed
2 zucchini, thickly sliced
2 large ripe tomatoes, peeled, seeded and chopped (see NOTE)
1/4 cup (7 g/1/4 oz) chopped fresh flat-leaf parsley
1 teaspoon seasoned pepper
150 g (5 oz) feta cheese, crumbled

BLACK OLIVE DRESSING
6 large marinated black olives, pitted
1/2 cup (125 ml/4 fl oz) olive oil
2 tablespoons balsamic vinegar

1 Cook the pasta in a large pan of rapidly boiling salted water until *al dente*. Drain well, spread in a single layer on a baking tray to dry, then refrigerate, uncovered, until chilled.
2 Cut the red and yellow capsicum into large pieces, removing the seeds and membrane. Place, skin-side-up, under a hot grill (broiler) until the skin blackens and blisters. Leave under a tea towel to cool, then peel away the skin. Slice the flesh into thick strips.
3 Heat the sunflower and olive oil in a frying pan. Add the garlic and eggplant and fry quickly, tossing, until lightly browned. Remove from the heat and place in a large bowl. Steam the zucchini for 1–2 minutes, or until just tender. Rinse under cold water, drain and add to the eggplant.
4 To make the dressing, process the olives in a food processor until finely chopped. Gradually add the olive oil, processing until thoroughly combined after each addition. Add the vinegar, season and process to combine.
5 Combine the pasta, capsicum, eggplant, zucchini, tomato, parsley and pepper in a large bowl. Top with the feta and drizzle with the dressing.

NUTRITION PER SERVE
Protein 15 g; Fat 55 g; Carbohydrate 50 g; Dietary Fibre 8 g; Cholesterol 25 mg; 3220 kJ (765 Cal)

NOTE: To peel tomatoes, score a cross in the base of each tomato. Leave in a pan of boiling water for 1 minute, then plunge into cold water. Peel the skin away from the cross. To remove the seeds, cut the tomato in half and scoop out the seeds with a teaspoon.

Drain the cooked pasta and spread on a tray to dry and cool.

Remove the seeds and white membrane from the capsicums and cut into large pieces.

Fry the garlic and cubed eggplant quickly until it is lightly browned.

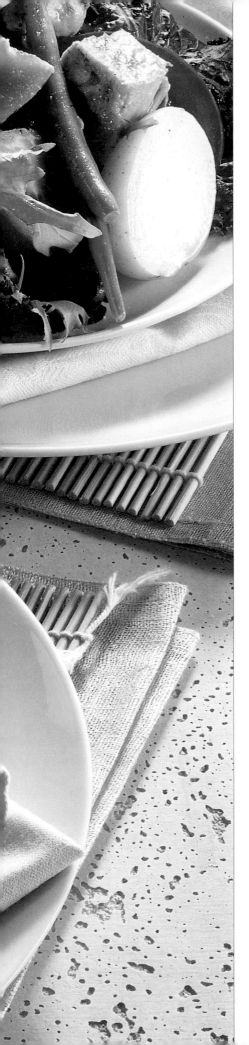

SEARED TUNA, POTATO AND BEAN SALAD

Preparation time: 10 minutes
Total cooking time: 20 minutes
Serves 4

12 baby new or small chat potatoes,
    or 250 g (8 oz) kipfler potatoes
150 g (5 oz) small green beans
2 x 200 g (6½ oz) tuna fillets
2 tablespoons olive oil
180 g (6 oz) mixed lettuce leaves
2 ripe tomatoes, cut into wedges
½ cup (60 g/2 oz) small black olives
4 hard-boiled eggs, quartered

DRESSING
2 tablespoons lemon juice
¼ cup (60 ml/2 fl oz) extra virgin
    olive oil
1 teaspoon Dijon mustard

1 Steam the whole potatoes in a steamer for 10 minutes, or until just tender (pierce with the point of a small sharp knife—if the potato comes away easily, it is ready). Drain thoroughly and keep warm.
2 Trim the beans and steam for 2 minutes. Drain and keep warm.
3 Brush the tuna fillets with oil and sprinkle both sides generously with freshly ground black pepper. Heat a chargrill or barbecue hotplate over high heat and brush with oil. Add the tuna and cook for 1–2 minutes on one side. Turn it over and cook the other side until seared on the outside. The tuna should still be pink in the centre. Remove the tuna, cool slightly, then cut into bite-sized cubes.
4 For the dressing, thoroughly whisk together the juice, oil and mustard in a large bowl. Season well.

5 To assemble the salad, divide the lettuce leaves among four serving plates. Cut the potatoes in half (if using kipfler, cut into thick slices). Put the potatoes, beans, tuna, tomatoes and olives in the dressing and toss gently. Spoon over the lettuce. Season well with salt and freshly ground black pepper and top with the egg quarters.

NUTRITION PER SERVE
Protein 33.5 g; Fat 35 g; Carbohydrate 12 g;
Dietary Fibre 4.5 g; Cholesterol 244 mg;
2095 kJ (500 Cal)

ALTERNATIVE FISH: Fresh salmon, canned tuna.
NOTE: Chat potatoes are small washed potatoes.
VARIATION: You can add chopped anchovies, capers and parsley to the dressing. If you find the flavour of anchovies too strong, chop them in a processor with all the dressing ingredients until smooth, then stir through as above.

Don't overcook the tuna. Just sear the outside—the centre should still be pink.

When cooled, cut the seared tuna into bite-sized cubes.

CHINESE ROAST DUCK, LIME, HERB AND NOODLE SALAD

Preparation time: 25 minutes +
  20 minutes soaking
Cooking time: 10 minutes
Serves 4

DRESSING
1/4 cup (60 ml/2 fl oz) fish sauce
2 tablespoons lime juice
1 tablespoon grated palm sugar
1 small red chilli, finely chopped

250 g (8 oz) dried flat rice stick
  noodles (5 mm/1/4 inch thick)
1 Chinese roast duck
1 tablespoon julienned ginger

90 g (3 1/4 oz) bean sprouts
1 small red onion, thinly sliced
3 tablespoons coriander leaves
3 tablespoons Thai basil or basil
1 lime, quartered

1 To make the dressing, combine the fish sauce, lime juice, palm sugar and chilli in a small bowl.
2 Place the noodles in a large bowl, cover with warm water and soak for 15–20 minutes, or until al dente. Drain, then return to the bowl.
3 Preheat the oven to moderate 180°C (350°F/Gas 4). Remove the flesh and skin from the duck in large pieces, then cut into thin strips. Place on a baking tray and heat in the oven for 10 minutes, or until the duck is warmed through.

4 Add the ginger, bean sprouts, onion, coriander, basil and the dressing to the noodles and toss until well combined. Serve the salad on a platter, or on individual serving plates or bowls, and arrange the duck strips on top. Serve with lime wedges.

NUTRITION PER SERVE
Protein 24.5 g; Fat 25.5 g; Carbohydrate 45.5 g;
Dietary Fibre 2.5 g; Cholesterol 115.5 mg;
2130 kJ (510 Cal)

NOTE: For crispy-skinned duck, place under a hot grill (broiler) for 1 minute, or until crisp. Arrange on the salad and serve immediately.

SOY CHICKEN AND GREEN TEA NOODLE SALAD

Preparation time: 30 minutes +
    cooling time + 2 hours marinating
Cooking time: 20 minutes
Serves 4–6

200 g (6¹/₂ oz) dried green tea soba
    noodles
2¹/₂ teaspoons sesame oil
2 chicken breast fillets (about 200 g/
    6¹/₂ oz each)
3 teaspoons grated ginger
¹/₃ cup (80 ml/2³/₄ fl oz) Japanese
    soy sauce
¹/₄ cup (60 ml/2 fl oz) mirin
1¹/₂ tablespoons sake
³/₄ teaspoon dashi granules
³/₄ teaspoon sugar
3 teaspoons rice vinegar
1 small Lebanese cucumber, cut in
    half lengthways and thinly sliced
1 tablespoon pickled ginger, shredded
2 spring onions, sliced on the diagonal
1 tablespoon black sesame seeds

1 Bring a large saucepan of water to the boil over high heat. Add the noodles and stir to separate. Return to the boil, then add 250 ml (1 cup) cold water. Repeat this step three times as the water just comes to the boil. Test a piece of soba—it should be tender to the bite, cooked through but not mushy. If it's not quite done, repeat one more time. Drain and rinse under cold water until the noodles are cold. Cut into 10 cm (4 inch) lengths using scissors. Toss with 2 teaspoons of the sesame oil.
2 Place the chicken in a non-metallic bowl. Combine the ginger, soy sauce, mirin, sake and the remaining sesame oil, then pour over the chicken and turn until well coated. Cover and refrigerate for 2 hours.
3 Line a bamboo steamer with baking paper. Remove the chicken, reserving the marinade and place the fillets in the steamer. Place the steamer over a wok or saucepan of simmering water, making sure the base doesn't touch the water. Cover and steam for 8–10 minutes, or until cooked

through. Remove and allow to cool completely.
4 Place the reserved marinade in a small saucepan with the dashi granules, sugar, rice vinegar and 90 ml (3 fl oz) water. Bring to the boil, then reduce the heat and simmer for 4–5 minutes. Remove and cool completely in the refrigerator.
5 Place the cucumber, pickled ginger, spring onion and noodles in a large bowl. Cut the chicken breasts into 5 mm (¹/₄ inch) strips on the diagonal. Add to the noodles. Pour on the dressing and toss well. Serve sprinkled with the sesame seeds.

NUTRITION PER SERVE (6)
Protein 19.5 g; Fat 6.5 g; Carbohydrate 25 g;
Dietary Fibre 1.5 g; Cholesterol 44 mg; 1040 kJ
(250 Cal)

NOTE: If green tea noodles (cha soba) are not available, plain soba noodles may be used instead. Both are available from Asian supermarkets.

VERMICELLI, BEEF AND THAI BASIL SALAD

Preparation time: 20 minutes
Total cooking time: 10–15 minutes
Serves 4

125 g (4 oz) dried rice vermicelli
600 g (1¼ lb) rump steak
oil, for cooking
2–3 cloves garlic, thinly sliced
1 small red chilli, finely chopped
1 small red capsicum, thinly
   sliced
1 red onion, thinly sliced
1 cup (30 g/1 oz) coriander leaves
1 cup (30 g/1 oz) Thai basil leaves or
   green basil leaves

DRESSING
1–2 cloves garlic, crushed
1 red chilli, chopped
2 tablespoons soy sauce
2 tablespoons lime juice
1 tablespoon fish sauce
3 tablespoons grated palm sugar

1 Soak the noodles in hot water for
5 minutes, or until soft. Drain.
2 Combine the dressing ingredients;
mix well and set aside.
3 Thinly slice the beef across the
grain. Heat the wok until very hot, add
1 tablespoon of the oil and swirl it
around to coat the side. Stir-fry the
beef in 2–3 batches for 2 minutes, or
until just brown, yet still pink in
patches. (Ensure the wok is hot before

each addition.) Remove all the beef
and set aside.
4 Heat another tablespoon of oil in
the wok, then stir-fry the garlic, chilli,
capsicum and onion for 2–3 minutes,
or until soft but not browned.
5 Add the beef to the wok to just heat
through quickly, then toss the mixture
through the vermicelli. Pour on the
dressing, and toss through the
coriander and Thai basil leaves.

NUTRITION PER SERVE
Protein 40 g; Fat 15 g; Carbohydrate 35 g;
Dietary Fibre 2 g; Cholesterol 100 mg;
1795 kJ (425 cal)

Slice the rump steak thinly across the grain, so it
holds together well.

Stir-fry the beef in batches so that it is just
beginning to turn brown.

Add the beef and toss through the vermicelli until
it is just heated through.

WARM MUSSEL AND POTATO SALAD

Preparation time: 20 minutes
Total cooking time: 20 minutes
Serves 4

500 g (1 lb) baby new potatoes
1 kg (2 lb) fresh black mussels
45 g (1¹/₂ oz) baby English spinach
    leaves

DRESSING
¹/₃ cup (80 ml/2³/₄ fl oz) olive oil
¹/₃ cup (80 ml/2³/₄ fl oz) cream
1 teaspoon grated lemon rind
2 tablespoons lemon juice
1 teaspoon caster sugar
1 tablespoon chopped lemon thyme

1 Cook the potatoes in boiling water until tender. Drain and keep warm.
2 Scrub the mussels well and remove the beards, discarding any that are open. Place in a pan with 2 cups (500 ml/16 fl oz) water, cover and cook gently until they have just opened. Do not overcook. Cover immediately with cold water and remove from the shells. Discard any mussels that have not opened. Pat dry with paper towels.
3 To make the dressing, put the oil, cream, lemon rind and juice, sugar and lemon thyme in a bowl and whisk to combine. Season with salt and pepper.
4 Combine the warm potatoes, mussels and spinach leaves in a large bowl. Add the dressing and toss gently. Serve immediately.

NUTRITION PER SERVE
Protein 45 g; Fat 35 g; Carbohydrate 20 g;
Dietary Fibre 2 g; Cholesterol 275 mg;
2310 kJ (550 Cal)

Grate a lemon on the fine side of a grater to get 1 teaspoon of grated rind.

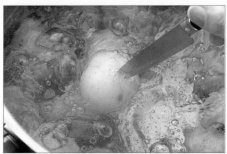

Cook the potatoes in boiling water until just tender.

Wash and scrub the mussels and remove the beards. Disard any that are open.

113

low fat

THAI-SPICED PORK AND GREEN MANGO SALAD

Preparation time: 45 minutes +
2 hours refrigeration
Total cooking time: 10 minutes
Serves 4

2 stems lemon grass (white part only),
thinly sliced
1 clove garlic
2 red Asian shallots
1 tablespoon coarsely chopped fresh
ginger
1 red bird's-eye chilli, seeded
1 tablespoon fish sauce
1/2 cup (15 g/1/2 oz) fresh coriander
1 teaspoon grated lime rind
1 tablespoon lime juice
2 tablespoons oil
2 pork tenderloins, trimmed

DRESSING
1 large red chilli, seeded and finely
chopped
2 cloves garlic, finely chopped
3 fresh coriander roots, finely chopped
11/4 tablespoons grated palm sugar
2 tablespoons fish sauce
1/4 cup (60 ml) lime juice

SALAD
2 green mangoes or 1 small green
papaya, peeled, pitted and cut into
julienne strips
1 carrot, grated
1/2 cup (45 g/11/2 oz) bean sprouts
1/2 red onion, thinly sliced
3 tablespoons roughly chopped fresh
mint
3 tablespoons roughly chopped fresh
coriander leaves
3 tablespoons roughly chopped fresh
Vietnamese mint

1 Place the lemon grass, garlic, shallots, ginger, chilli, fish sauce, coriander, lime rind, lime juice and oil in a blender or food processor and process until a coarse paste forms. Transfer to a non-metallic dish. Coat the pork in the marinade, cover and refrigerate for at least 2 hours, but no longer than 4 hours.
2 To make the salad dressing, mix all the ingredients together in a bowl.

3 Combine all the salad ingredients in a large bowl.
4 Preheat a grill (broiler) or chargrill pan and cook the pork over medium heat for 4–5 minutes each side, or until cooked through. Remove from the heat, and then leave to rest for 5 minutes before slicing to serve.
5 Toss the dressing and salad together. Season to taste with salt and

cracked black pepper. Arrange the sliced pork in a circle in the centre of each plate and top with salad. Delicious with steamed jasmine rice.

NUTRITION PER SERVE
Protein 60 g; Fat 14 g; Carbohydrate 20 g;
Dietary Fibre 3 g; Cholesterol 122 mg;
1860 kJ (444 Cal)

Mix the marinade ingredients to a coarse paste in a processor or blender.

Cook the pork under the grill or in a chargrill pan until it is cooked through.

CHICKEN, PRAWN AND GRAPEFRUIT SALAD

Preparation time: 20 minutes
Total cooking time: Nil
Serves 4–6

1 small pink or yellow grapefruit
1/2 small green pawpaw or green
    mango (about 100 g/3 1/2 oz)
6 cooked prawns, peeled and
    deveined
2 Roma tomatoes, chopped
1 orange, peeled and segmented
125 g (4 oz) cooked chicken,
    shredded or cut into bite-sized
    pieces (see Note)
4 spring onions, sliced
2 cloves garlic, sliced
2 tablespoons coarsely chopped fresh
    coriander
1 tablespoon shredded coconut
lettuce leaves, to serve
1 tablespoon roasted, unsalted
    peanuts, finely chopped
2 teaspoons dried shrimp, finely
    chopped

DRESSING
2 teaspoons soft brown sugar
1 1/2 tablespoons fish sauce
1/4 cup (60 ml/2 fl oz) lime juice
2 teaspoons chilli sauce

1 Peel the grapefruit, discarding the pith, then cut it into thin segments. Peel the pawpaw and cut it into long, thin strips.
2 Combine the pawpaw, grapefruit, prawns, tomato, orange segments, chicken, spring onion, garlic, coriander and coconut in a bowl.
3 To make the dressing, combine the sugar, fish sauce, lime juice and chilli sauce in a jug and whisk until the sugar has dissolved. Pour the dressing over the salad and toss gently. Serve on a bed of lettuce leaves and sprinkle with the peanuts and dried shrimp.

NUTRITION PER SERVE (6)
Protein 9.5 g; Fat 1.5 g; Carbohydrate 8.5 g;
Dietary Fibre 2.5 g; Cholesterol 34 mg;
376 kJ (98 cal)

NOTE: Use leftover chicken, or pan-fry a chicken breast until tender.

Peel the grapefruit, removing all the white pith. Cut into thin segments.

Cut the peeled pawpaw into long, thin strips, using a sharp knife.

Combine the fruit, chicken, tomato, spring onion, garlic, coriander, coconut and prawns in a bowl.

Whisk the dressing ingredients in a small jug until the sugar has dissolved.

TANDOORI LAMB SALAD

Preparation time: 20 minutes
 + overnight marinating
Total cooking time: 15 minutes
Serves 4 as a light lunch or starter

1 cup (250 g/8 oz) low-fat natural
   yoghurt
2 cloves garlic, crushed
2 teaspoons grated fresh ginger
2 teaspoons ground turmeric
2 teaspoons garam masala
1/4 teaspoon paprika
2 teaspoons ground coriander

red food colouring, optional
500 g (1 lb) lean lamb fillets
4 tablespoons lemon juice
1 1/2 teaspoons chopped fresh
   coriander
1 teaspoon chopped fresh mint
150 g (5 oz) mixed salad leaves
1 large mango, cut into strips
2 cucumbers, cut into matchsticks

1 Mix the yoghurt, garlic, ginger and
spices in a bowl, add a little colouring
and toss with the lamb to thoroughly
coat. Cover and refrigerate overnight.
2 Grill (broil) the lamb on a foil-lined
baking tray under high heat for

7 minutes each side, or until the
marinade starts to brown. Set aside
for 5 minutes before serving.
3 Mix the lemon juice, coriander and
mint, then season. Toss with the salad
leaves, mango and cucumber, then
arrange on plates. Slice the lamb and
serve over the salad.

NUTRITION PER SERVE
Protein 30 g; Fat 6.5 g; Carbohydrate 8 g;
Dietary Fibre 2 g; Cholesterol 90 mg;
965 kJ (230 Cal)

Coat the lamb with the marinade, cover and
refrigerate overnight.

Cut the mango flesh into long, thin strips, using a
sharp knife.

Turn the lamb after about 7 minutes and cook
until the marinade starts to brown.

WARM TUNA AND CORIANDER NOODLE SALAD

Preparation time: 15 minutes
Total cooking time: 10 minutes
Serves 4

1/4 cup (60 ml/2 fl oz) lime juice
2 tablespoons fish sauce
2 tablespoons sweet chilli sauce
2 teaspoons grated palm sugar
1 teaspoon sesame oil
1 clove garlic, finely chopped
1 tablespoon virgin olive oil
4 tuna steaks
200 g (6¹/₂ oz) dried thin wheat noodles

6 spring onions, thinly sliced
³/₄ cup (25 g/³/₄ oz) chopped fresh coriander leaves
lime wedges, to garnish

1 To make the dressing, place the lime juice, fish sauce, chilli sauce, sugar, sesame oil and garlic in a small bowl and mix together.
2 Heat the olive oil in a chargrill pan or barbecue hotplate. Add the tuna steaks and cook over high heat for 2 minutes each side, or until cooked to your liking. Transfer the steaks to a warm plate, cover and keep warm.
3 Place the noodles in a large saucepan of lightly salted, rapidly boiling water and return to the boil.

Cook for 4 minutes, or until the noodles are tender. Drain well. Add half the dressing and half the spring onion and coriander to the noodles and gently toss together.
4 Either cut the tuna into even cubes or slice it.
5 Place the noodles on serving plates and top with the tuna. Mix the remaining dressing with the spring onion and coriander and drizzle over the tuna. Garnish with lime wedges.

NUTRITION PER SERVE
Protein 32 g; Fat 10 g; Carbohydrate 5 g;
Dietary Fibre 1 g; Cholesterol 105 mg;
1030 kJ (245 Cal)

Cook the tuna steaks in a chargrill pan until cooked to your liking.

Cook the noodles in lightly salted water until they are tender.

Combine the remaining dressing with the spring onion and coriander.

119

CHARGRILLED CHICKEN SALAD

Preparation time: 20 minutes
  + 2 hours marinating
Total cooking time: 1 hour
Serves 4

4 chicken breast fillets
2 tablespoons honey
1 tablespoon wholegrain mustard
1 tablespoon soy sauce
2 red onions, cut into wedges
8 Roma tomatoes, halved lengthways
2 tablespoons soft brown sugar
2 tablespoons balsamic vinegar
cooking oil spray
snow pea sprouts, for serving

1 Preheat the oven to moderate 180°C (350°F/Gas 4). Trim the chicken of any excess fat and place in a shallow dish. Combine the honey, mustard and soy sauce and pour over the chicken, tossing to coat. Cover and refrigerate for 2 hours, turning once.
2 Place the onion wedges and tomato halves on a baking tray covered with baking paper. Sprinkle with the sugar and drizzle with the balsamic vinegar. Bake for 40 minutes.
3 Heat a chargrill pan or barbecue hotplate and lightly spray with oil. Remove the chicken from the marinade and cook for 4–5 minutes on each side, or until cooked through. Slice the chicken and serve with the snow pea sprouts, tomato halves and onion wedges.

NUTRITION PER SERVE
Protein 25 g; Fat 2.5 g; Carbohydrate 30 g; Dietary Fibre 3 g; Cholesterol 50 mg; 990 kJ (235 Cal)

Pour the marinade over the chicken and toss to coat thoroughly.

Drizzle the balsamic vinegar over the onion wedges and tomato halves.

Cook the marinated chicken in a hot, lightly oiled chargrill pan.

TOFU SALAD WITH GINGER MISO DRESSING

Preparation time: 20 minutes +
  overnight marinating
Total cooking time: 5 minutes
Serves 4

90 ml (3 fl oz) light soy sauce
2 teaspoons soy bean oil
2 cloves garlic, crushed
1 teaspoon grated fresh ginger
1 teaspoon chilli paste
500 g (1 lb) firm tofu, cut into small
  cubes
400 g (13 oz) mesclun leaves
1 Lebanese cucumber, finely sliced
250 g (8 oz) cherry tomatoes, halved
2 teaspoons soy bean oil, extra

DRESSING
2 teaspoons white miso paste (see
  NOTE)
2 tablespoons mirin
1 teaspoon sesame oil
1 teaspoon grated fresh ginger
1 teaspoon finely chopped chives
1 tablespoon toasted sesame seeds

1 Mix together the tamari, soy bean oil, garlic, ginger, chilli paste and $1/2$ teaspoon salt in a bowl. Add the tofu and mix until well coated. Marinate for at least 10 minutes, or preferably overnight. Drain and reserve the marinade.
2 To make the dressing, combine the miso with $1/2$ cup (125 ml/4 fl oz) hot water and leave until the miso dissolves. Add the mirin, sesame oil, ginger, chives and sesame seeds and stir tuntil beginning to thicken.
3 Put the mesclun leaves, cucumber and tomato in a serving bowl.
4 Heat the extra soy bean oil on a chargrill or barbecue hotplate. Add the tofu and cook over medium heat for 4 minutes, or until golden brown. Pour on the reserved marinade and cook for a further 1 minute over high heat. Remove from the grill and cool for 5 minutes.
5 Add the tofu to the salad, drizzle with the dressing and toss well.

NUTRITION PER SERVE
Protein 12 g; Fat 8 g; Carbohydrate 4 g; Dietary Fibre 4 g; Cholesterol 0 mg; 590 kJ (140 Cal)

NOTE: Miso is Japanese bean paste and is commonly used in soups, dressings, on grilled foods and as a flavouring for pickles.

Gently stir the tofu cubes through the marinade until well coated.

Stir the dressing ingredients together until it begins to thicken.

Cook the tofu cubes over medium heat until each side is golden brown.

VIETNAMESE PAWPAW AND CHICKEN SALAD

Preparation time: 30 minutes
Total cooking time: 10 minutes
Serves 4

2 chicken breast fillets (350 g/11 oz)
1 large green pawpaw
1 cup (20 g/³/₄ oz) fresh Vietnamese
 mint leaves
¹/₂ cup (15 g/¹/₂ oz) fresh coriander
 leaves
2 red chillies, seeded and thinly sliced
2 tablespoons fish sauce
1 tablespoon rice wine vinegar
1 tablespoon lime juice
2 teaspoons sugar
2 tablespoons chopped roasted
 peanuts

1 Place the chicken in a frying pan with enough water to just cover. Simmer over gentle heat for 10 minutes, or until cooked. Don't let the water boil—it should just gently simmer, to poach the chicken. Remove the chicken and allow to cool completely. Thinly slice the chicken.
2 Using a potato peeler, peel the pawpaw and then cut the flesh into thin strips. Mix gently in a bowl with the mint, coriander, sliced chilli, fish sauce, vinegar, lime juice and sugar.
3 Arrange the pawpaw mixture on a serving plate and pile the sliced chicken on top. Scatter the peanuts over the top and serve immediately.

NUTRITION PER SERVE
Protein 22 g; Fat 6 g; Carbohydrate 6 g;
Dietary Fibre 1.5 g; Cholesterol 44 mg;
712 kJ (170 cal)

NOTE: Green pawpaw is underripe pawpaw, used for tartness and texture.

Gently simmer the chicken breast fillets until they are cooked through.

Use a sharp knife to cut the cooled chicken into thin slices.

Cut the peeled pawpaw into long, thin strips, using a very sharp knife.

GRILLED CAPSICUM AND ANCHOVY PASTA SALAD

Preparation time: 15 minutes
Total cooking time: 25 minutes
Serves 4–6

500 g (1 lb) penne or spiral pasta
2 large red capsicums
1 small red onion, finely chopped
1 cup (30 g/1 oz) fresh flat-leaf parsley
   leaves
2 anchovies, whole or chopped
3 tablespoons olive oil
2 tablespoons lemon juice

1 Cook the pasta in a large pan of rapidly boiling salted water until *al dente*. Drain and rinse under cold water.
2 Cut the capsicum into large pieces, removing the seeds and membrane. Place cut-side-down under a hot grill (broiler) and cook for 8 minutes or until the skin is blistered and black. Cover with a tea towel and leave to cool, then peel away the skin and cut the flesh into thin strips.
3 Toss together the pasta, capsicum, onion, parsley, anchovies, oil, lemon juice and some salt and pepper. Serve immediately.

NUTRITION PER SERVE (6)
Protein 11 g; Fat 11 g; Carbohydrate 62 g;
Dietary Fibre 7 g; Cholesterol 0 mg;
1640 kJ (400 Cal)

HINT: The capsicum can be peeled a day in advance, covered well and then refrigerated. Removing the skin in this way results in a much sweeter taste.

Cut the red onion in half and then use a sharp knife to finely chop.

Remvoe the seeds and membrane from the capsicum before grilling.

Put all the ingredients in a large bowl and toss together well.

FARFALLE SALAD WITH SUN-DRIED TOMATOES AND SPINACH

Preparation time: 20 minutes
Total cooking time: 15 minutes
Serves 4–6

500 g (1 lb) farfalle or spiral pasta
3 spring onions
60 g (2 oz) sun-dried tomatoes, cut into strips
500 g (1 lb) English spinach, trimmed and shredded
1/3 cup (50 g/1 3/4 oz) pine nuts, toasted
1 tablespoon chopped fresh oregano

DRESSING
3 tablespoons olive oil
1 teaspoon fresh chopped chilli
1 clove garlic, crushed

1 Cook the pasta in a large pan of rapidly boiling salted water until *al dente*. Drain well and rinse under cold water. Transfer to a large salad bowl. Trim the spring onions and chop finely. Add to the pasta with the tomato, spinach, pine nuts and fresh oregano.

2 To make the dressing, put the oil, chilli and garlic in a small screw-top jar and add salt and pepper to taste. Shake well.

3 Pour the dressing over the salad, toss well and serve immediately.

NUTRITION PER SERVE (6)
Protein 12 g; Fat 8 g; Carbohydrate 60 g;
Dietary Fibre 6 g; Cholesterol 0 mg;
1490 kJ (357 Cal)

Put the dressing ingredients in a screw-top jar so you can mix them together by shaking.

Pour the dressing over the salad and then toss together before serving.

SCALLOPS AND GREEN PEPPERCORN SALAD

Preparation time: 20 minutes +
  20 minutes marinating
Total cooking time: 5 minutes
Serves 4

1/4 cup (60 ml/2 fl oz) olive oil
2 teaspoons green peppercorns,
  chopped

2 teaspoons finely grated lime rind
1 teaspoon finely grated fresh ginger
500 g (1 lb) scallops with corals,
  deveined
salad leaves and pickled ginger, to
  serve

1 Combine the oil, peppercorns, rind and fresh ginger. Add the scallops and refrigerate for 20 minutes.
2 Cook the scallops on a very hot, lightly oiled barbecue flatplate, in

batches, stirring gently, for about
2 minutes, or until they become lightly golden brown.
3 Serve the scallops on salad leaves and topped with ginger strips.

NUTRITION PER SERVE
Protein 15 g; Fat 15 g; Carbohydrate 1 g;
Dietary Fibre 0 g; Cholesterol 40 mg;
820 kJ (195 Cal)

Peel the skin from the fresh ginger and finely grate the flesh.

Mix together the oil, peppercorns, lime rind and ginger to make a marinade.

Cook the scallops on a very hot barbecue flatplate until they are lightly golden brown.

SUMMER SALAD WITH BASIL DRESSING

Preparation time: 15 minutes
Total cooking time: 5 minutes
Serves 8

2 carrots
6 radishes
150 g (5 oz) snow peas
250 g (8 oz) asparagus
1 cup (30 g/1 oz) fresh basil leaves
½ cup (125 ml/4 fl oz) olive oil
1 tablespoon white wine vinegar
½ teaspoon French mustard
¼ teaspoon sugar

1 Thinly slice the carrots and radishes. Trim the ends from the snow peas and cut into short lengths. Snap the woody ends from the asparagus and put in a pan with a small amount of water.
2 Cook the asparagus over low heat until just tender. Plunge into cold water and then drain and pat dry with paper towels.
3 Put the basil in a food processor and blend until finely chopped. Add the oil, vinegar, mustard and sugar and process until smooth. Store in a screw-top jar until required. Put the vegetables in a large serving bowl and toss together. Add the dressing and toss well.

NUTRITION PER SERVE
Protein 2 g; Fat 15 g; Carbohydrate 4 g;
Dietary Fibre 2 g; Cholesterol 0 mg;
650 kJ (156 cal)

STORAGE: The dressing can be kept in the fridge for up to 2 days.

VARIATION: Make the dressing with fresh coriander instead of basil.

Cut the radishes and carrots into thin slices and cut the snow peas into short lengths.

Plunge the asparagus into cold water to stop the cooking and dry with paper towels.

Blend the basil leaves until finely chopped, then add the other dressing ingredients.

SALT-AND-PEPPER SQUID SALAD

Preparation time: 40 minutes
  + 20 minutes marinating
Total cooking time: 10 minutes
Serves 4

500 g (1 lb) squid tubes
1/3 cup (80 ml/2³/₄ fl oz) oil
4 cloves garlic, finely chopped
1/2 teaspoon sugar
2 teaspoons sea salt
1 teaspoon ground black pepper
150 g (5 oz) baby English spinach
  leaves
100 g (3¹/₂ oz) cherry tomatoes,
  quartered
2 tablespoons lime juice
lime quarters, to garnish

1 Cut the squid tubes in half lengthways and open them out. Rinse and pat dry with paper towels. Lay on a chopping board with the inside facing upwards. Honeycomb the squid by scoring along the length of each piece very finely, then diagonally across the width to create a fine diamond pattern. Cut the squid into pieces 5 x 3 cm (2 x 1¹/₄ inches). Combine the squid, oil, garlic, sugar and half the salt and pepper, cover and refrigerate for 20 minutes.

2 Arrange the spinach leaves and tomatoes on a large serving platter.

3 Heat the wok until it is very hot and stir-fry the squid over high heat in several batches, tossing constantly, for 1–2 minutes, or until the squid just turns white and curls. Keep the wok very hot and don't cook the squid for too long or it will toughen.

4 Return all the squid pieces to the wok with the lime juice and the remaining salt and pepper. Stir briefly until heated through. Arrange on top of the spinach and garnish with the lime wedges. Serve immediately.

NUTRITION PER SERVE
Protein 20 g; Fat 15 g; Carbohydrate 3 g;
Dietary Fibre 2 g; Cholesterol 250 mg;
1020 kJ (250 Cal)

Cut the squid tubes in half lengthways, and open them out.

Score very finely along the length, then diagonally to create a diamond pattern.

Fold the honeycombed squid tubes over and cut them into pieces.

Stir-fry the squid in batches until it turns white and curls up. Take care not to overcook.

PRAWN SALAD WITH KAFFIR LIME

Preparation time: 35 minutes
Total cooking time: 2 minutes
Serves 4

200 g (6¹/₂ oz) baby green beans
2 Lebanese cucumbers, sliced
4 spring onions, finely chopped
1 tablespoon finely shredded kaffir
   lime leaves
¹/₄ cup (15 g/¹/₂ oz) flaked coconut
750 g (1¹/₂ lb) cooked prawns,
   peeled, tails intact
2 teaspoons shredded lime rind

DRESSING
1 tablespoon peanut oil
1 tablespoon nam pla (Thai fish sauce)
1 tablespoon grated palm sugar
1 tablespoon chopped fresh coriander
2 teaspoons soy sauce
1–2 teaspoons sweet chilli sauce
¹/₄ cup (60 ml/2 fl oz) lime juice

1 Cook the beans in a small pan of boiling water for 2 minutes. Drain and cover with cold water, then drain again and pat dry with paper towels.
2 To make the dressing, whisk the ingredients in a bowl.
3 Combine the beans, cucumber, spring onion, lime leaves, flaked coconut and prawns in a large bowl. Add the dressing and toss gently to combine. Place the salad in a large serving bowl and garnish with the shredded lime rind.

NUTRITION PER SERVE
Protein 45 g; Fat 8 g; Carbohydrate 7 g;
Dietary Fibre 3 g; Cholesterol 350 mg;
1200 kJ (285 Cal)

NOTE: Young lemon leaves can be used in place of the kaffir lime leaves if they are not available.

Soft brown or dark brown sugar may be substituted for the palm sugar.

Cut the cucumbers in half lengthways, then cut into slices.

Lower the beans into a small pan of boiling water and cook for 2 minutes.

Whisk the dressing ingredients in a small bowl until combined.

SPICY LENTIL SALAD

Preparation time: 30 minutes
Total cooking time: 1 hour 10 minutes
Serves 6

1 cup (220 g/7 oz) brown rice
1 cup (185 g/6 oz) brown lentils
1 teaspoon turmeric
1 teaspoon ground cinnamon
6 cardamom pods
3 star anise
2 bay leaves
1/4 cup (60 ml/2 fl oz) sunflower oil
1 tablespoon lemon juice
250 g (8 oz) broccoli florets
2 carrots, cut into julienne strips
1 onion, finely chopped
2 cloves garlic, crushed
1 red capsicum, finely chopped
1 teaspoon garam masala
1 teaspoon ground coriander
1 1/2 cups (250 g/8 oz) fresh or frozen
    peas, thawed

MINT AND YOGHURT DRESSING
1 cup (250 g/8 oz) plain yoghurt
1 tablespoon lemon juice
1 tablespoon chopped fresh mint
1 teaspoon cumin seeds

1 Put 3 cups (750 ml/24 fl oz) water with the rice, lentils, turmeric, cinnamon, cardamom, star anise and bay leaves in a pan. Stir well and bring to the boil. Reduce the heat, cover and simmer gently for 50–60 minutes, or until the liquid is absorbed. Remove the whole spices. Transfer the mixture to a large bowl. Whisk 2 tablespoons of the oil with the lemon juice and fork through the rice mixture.
2 Boil, steam or microwave the broccoli and carrots until tender. Drain and refresh in cold water.

3 Heat the remaining oil in a large pan and add the onion, garlic and capsicum. Stir-fry for 2–3 minutes, then add the garam masala and coriander, and stir-fry for a further 1–2 minutes. Add the vegetables and toss to coat in the spice mixture. Add to the rice and fork through to combine. Cover and refrigerate until cold.
4 To make the dressing, mix the

yoghurt, lemon juice, mint and cumin seeds together, and season with salt and pepper. Spoon the salad into individual serving bowls or onto a platter and serve with the dressing.

NUTRITION PER SERVE
Protein 20 g; Fat 15 g; Carbohydrate 50 g;
Dietary Fibre 10 g; Cholesterol 7 mg;
1605 kJ (380 cal)

Add the cardamom pods, star anise and bay leaves to the pan.

Add the vegetables and toss to coat with the spice mixture.

Mix the yoghurt, lemon juice, mint and cumin seeds together to make a dressing.

CHARGRILLED TUNA AND RUBY GRAPEFRUIT SALAD

Preparation time: 20 minutes
Total cooking time: 10 minutes
Serves 6

4 ruby grapefruit
cooking oil spray
3 tuna steaks
150 g (5 oz) rocket
    leaves
1 red onion, sliced

ALMOND AND RASPBERRY
    DRESSING
2 tablespoons almond oil
2 tablespoons raspberry vinegar
1/2 teaspoon sugar
1 tablespoon shredded fresh mint

1 Cut a slice off each end of the grapefruit and peel away the skin, removing all the pith. Separate the segments and set aside in a bowl.
2 Heat a chargrill or barbecue hotplate and spray lightly with oil. Cook each tuna steak for 3–4 minutes on each side. This will leave the centre slightly pink. Cool, then thinly slice or flake.
3 To make the dressing, put the almond oil, vinegar, sugar and mint in a small screw-top jar and shake until well combined.
4 Place the rocket on a serving plate and top with the grapefruit segments, then the tuna and onion. Drizzle with the dressing and serve.

NUTRITION PER SERVE
Protein 15 g; Fat 7 g; Carbohydrate 8 g;
Dietary Fibre 2 g; Cholesterol 50 mg;
1015 kJ (240 Cal)

Cut a slice off the ends of the grapefruit and peel away the skin and pith.

Separate the grapefruit into segments and set aside in a bowl.

Cook the tuna steaks on a lightly oiled chargrill plate—they should still be pink in the centre.

TOMATO PASTA SALAD WITH THAI-STYLE VEGETABLES

Preparation time: 20 minutes
Total cooking time: 20 minutes
Serves 4–6

350 g (11 oz) tomato fettucine or plain fettucine
100 g (3¹/₂ oz) fresh baby corn, halved lengthways
1 carrot, cut into julienne strips (see NOTE)
200 g (6¹/₂ oz) broccoli, cut into small florets

¹/₂ red capsicum, cut into julienne strips
2 teaspoons sesame seeds
3 spring onions, chopped

DRESSING
¹/₄ cup (60 ml/2 fl oz) sweet chilli sauce
2 teaspoons fish sauce
¹/₄ cup (90 g/3 oz) honey

1 Cook the pasta in a large pan of rapidly boiling salted water until *al dente*. Drain well and cool.
2 Cook the corn in boiling water for 1 minute. Remove and plunge into a bowl of iced water. Cook the carrot, broccoli and capsicum in boiling water for 30 seconds, then drain and add to the iced water to cool. Drain the vegetables and add to the pasta.
3 To make the dressing, whisk the ingredients together, drizzle over the salad and toss well. Sprinkle with the sesame seeds and spring onions.

NUTRITION PER SERVE (6)
Protein 10 g; Fat 1 g; Carbohydrate 60 g;
Dietary Fibre 6 g; Cholesterol 0 mg;
1260 kJ (300 cal)

NOTE: Julienne strips are even-sized strips of vegetables, cut to the size and shape of matchsticks.

Cut the broccoli into small florets and the other vegetables into strips.

Cook the carrot, broccoli and capsicum in boiling water for 30 seconds.

Whisk together the sweet chilli sauce, fish sauce and honey.

SPICY FUN SEE NOODLE SALAD

Preparation time: 20 minutes +
    5 minutes soaking + 2 hours
    refrigeration
Total cooking time: 5 minutes
Serves 4

125 g (4 oz) mung bean vermicelli
    (fun see)
1 teaspoon sesame oil
1 large carrot, julienned
2 sticks celery, julienned
100 g (3½ oz) snow peas, julienned
2 small Lebanese cucumbers
3 spring onions, thinly sliced into long
    diagonal strips
½ cup (15 g/½ oz) fresh coriander
    leaves
½ cup (10 g/¼ oz) fresh mint

DRESSING
⅓ cup (70 g/2 oz) Chinese sesame
    paste

2 teaspoons chilli oil
¼ cup (60 ml/2 fl oz) light soy sauce
1 tablespoon white vinegar
1 tablespoon sugar
¼ teaspoon cayenne pepper
2½ tablespoons chicken stock

1 Place the noodles in a large heatproof bowl, cover with boiling water and soak for 3–4 minutes, or until softened. Drain. Cut in half with scissors, place in a large bowl, add the sesame oil and mix well. Cover and refrigerate for 1 hour, or until needed.
2 Bring a large saucepan of water to the boil, add the carrot, celery, snow peas and 2 teaspoons salt and cook for 30 seconds. Drain and refresh in icy cold water. Drain again and pat dry, making sure that as little moisture as possible remains. Seed and julienne the cucumber, and combine with the vegetables and spring onion. Refrigerate for 1 hour.
3 To make the dressing, place the sesame paste in a bowl and stir well.

Slowly mix in the chilli oil, soy sauce, vinegar, sugar, cayenne pepper and chicken stock.
4 Just before serving, add three quarters of the blanched vegetables and three quarters of the herbs to the chilled noodles. Pour the dressing on top, then toss well. Season to taste with salt and pepper. Transfer to a serving platter and top with the remaining vegetables and herbs.

NUTRITION PER SERVE
Protein 6 g; Fat 13 g; Carbohydrate 25.5 g;
Dietary Fibre 6.5 g; Cholesterol 0 mg;
1020 kJ (245 Cal)

INDIAN-STYLE LAMB COUSCOUS SALAD

Preparation time: 25 minutes
Total cooking time: 35 minutes
Serves 6

250 g (8 oz) lamb backstrap
   (tender eye of the lamb loin)
1 tablespoon mild curry powder
2 tablespoons pepitas
   (pumpkin seeds)
2 tablespoons sesame seeds
2 teaspoons cumin seeds
2 teaspoons coriander seeds
1 tablespoon oil
2 tablespoons lemon juice
1 onion, chopped
1 carrot, chopped
125 g (4 oz) orange sweet potato,
   cubed
1 clove garlic, finely chopped
1 cup (185 g/6 oz) couscous
1/4 cup (50 g/1 3/4 oz) raisins

1 Sprinkle the lamb with the combined curry powder and a pinch of salt, then turn to coat well. Cover with plastic wrap and refrigerate while preparing the salad.

2 Place the pepitas and sesame seeds in a dry frying pan and cook, stirring, over medium-high heat until the seeds begin to brown. Add the cumin and coriander seeds and continue stirring until the pepitas are puffed and begin to pop. Remove from the heat and allow to cool.

3 Heat the oil in a pan, add the lamb and cook over medium-high heat for 5–8 minutes, or until browned and tender. Remove from the pan, drizzle with half the lemon juice and leave to cool to room temperature. Turn the meat occasionally to coat in the lemon juice while cooling.

4 Using the same pan, stir the onion, carrot and sweet potato over high heat until the onion is translucent. Reduce the heat to medium, add 3 tablespoons water, cover and cook for about 3 minutes, or until the vegetables are tender. Stir in the chopped garlic and remaining lemon juice.

5 Pour 1 cup (250 ml/8 fl oz) boiling water into a heatproof bowl and add the couscous. Stir until combined. Leave for about 2 minutes, or until the water has been absorbed. Fluff gently with a fork to separate the grains. Add the vegetable mixture, raisins and most of the toasted nuts and seeds, reserving some to sprinkle over the top, and toss until just combined. Spoon the mixture onto a serving plate. Slice the lamb thinly and arrange over the salad. Drizzle with any leftover lemon juice and sprinkle with the nuts and seeds.

NUTRITION PER SERVE
Protein 15 g; Fat 10 g; Carbohydrate 30 g;
Dietary Fibre 3 g; Cholesterol 30 mg;
1135 kJ (270 Cal)

Sprinkle the lamb backstrap with the combined curry powder and salt.

Fry the seeds in a dry frying pan until the pepitas puff up.

When the water has been absorbed, fluff the couscous gently with a fork.

CHICKPEA SALAD WITH TAHINI DRESSING

Preparation time: 20 minutes
Total cooking time: Nil
Serves 8

2 large cans chickpeas (see NOTE)
3 tomatoes
1 red onion, thinly sliced
1 small red capsicum, cut into thin
    strips
4 spring onions, cut into thin strips
1 cup (60 g/2 oz) chopped fresh
    parsley
2–3 tablespoons chopped fresh mint
    leaves

DRESSING
2 tablespoons tahini (sesame paste)
2 tablespoons fresh lemon juice
3 tablespoons olive oil
2 cloves garlic, crushed
1/2 teaspoon ground cumin

1 Drain the chickpeas and rinse well.
Cut the tomatoes in half and remove
the seeds with a spoon. Dice the flesh.
Mix the onion, tomato, capsicum and
spring onion in a bowl. Add the
chickpeas, parsley and mint.
2 To make the dressing, put all the
ingredients in a screw-top jar with
2 tablespoons water, season well and
shake vigorously to make a creamy
liquid. Pour over the salad and toss.

NUTRITION PER SERVE
Protein 4 g; Fat 2 g; Carbohydrate 8 g;
Dietary Fibre 3 g; Cholesterol 0 mg;
877 kJ (210 Cal)

STORAGE: Can be kept, covered, in
the fridge for up to 3 hours.

NOTE: You can also use dried
chickpeas, but they will need to be
soaked and cooked first. Use 13/4 cups
(380 g/12 oz) dried chickpeas and
put in a pan with 3.5 litres (112 fl oz)
water and 3 tablespoons olive oil.
Partially cover and boil for 21/2 hours,
or until tender. Rinse, drain well and
allow to cool a little before making
the salad.

Both canned and dried chickpeas should be
rinsed and drained well.

Cut the tomatoes in half and scoop out the
seeds with a teaspoon.

The easiest way to make a salad dressing is by
shaking the ingredients in a screw-top jar.

ASIAN CHICKEN SALAD

Preparation time: 25 minutes
Total cooking time: 10 minutes
Serves 6

1 small Chinese cabbage, finely
　shredded
2 tablespoons oil
2 onions, halved and sliced thinly
500 g (1 lb) chicken thigh fillets,
　trimmed and cut into strips
1/4 cup (60 g/2 oz) sugar
1/4 cup (60 ml/2 fl oz) fish sauce

1/3 cup (80 ml/2³/4 fl oz) lime juice
1 tablespoon white vinegar
2/3 cup (30 g/1 oz) chopped
　Vietnamese mint or common mint
2/3 cup (30 g) chopped coriander
Vietnamese mint leaves, extra, to
　garnish

1　Place the cabbage in a large bowl,
cover with plastic wrap and chill.
2　Heat a wok until very hot, add
1 tablespoon oil and swirl to coat. Add
half the onion and half the chicken,
and stir-fry for 4–5 minutes, or until
the chicken is cooked through.

Remove and repeat with the remaining
oil, onion and chicken. Cool.
3　To make the dressing, mix together
the sugar, fish sauce, lime juice,
vinegar and 1/2 teaspoon salt with a
fork. To serve, toss together the
cabbage, chicken and onion, dressing,
mint and coriander and garnish with
the mint leaves.

NUTRITION PER SERVE
Protein 17 g; Fat 8 g; Carbohydrate 13 g;
Dietary Fibre 1.5 g; Cholesterol 35 mg;
805 kJ (190 Cal)

Finely shred the small Chinese cabbage and then
leave to chill.

Stir-fry half the onion and half the chicken strips
for 4–5 minutes.

Mix together the dressing ingredients with a fork,
then toss with the salad.

PESTO BEEF SALAD

Preparation time: 30 minutes
Total cooking time: 25 minutes
Serves 8 as a starter

100 g (3¹/2 oz) button mushrooms
1 large yellow capsicum
1 large red capsicum
cooking oil spray
100 g (3¹/2 oz) lean fillet steak
1¹/2 cups (135 g/4¹/2 oz) penne

PESTO
1 cup (50 g/1³/4 oz) tightly packed
    basil leaves
2 cloves garlic, chopped
2 tablespoons pepitas (pumpkin seeds)

1 tablespoon olive oil
2 tablespoons orange juice
1 tablespoon lemon juice

1 Cut the mushrooms into quarters. Cut the capsicums into large flat pieces, removing the seeds and membrane. Place skin-side-up under a hot grill (broiler) until blackened. Leave covered with a tea towel until cool, then peel away the skin and chop the flesh.

2 Spray a non-stick frying pan with oil and cook the steak over high heat for 3–4 minutes each side until it is medium-rare. Remove and leave for 5 minutes before cutting into thin slices. Season with a little salt.

3 To make the pesto, finely chop the basil leaves, garlic and pepitas in a food processor. With the motor running, add the oil, orange and lemon juice. Season well.

4 Meanwhile, cook the penne in a large pan of rapidly boiling salted water until *al dente*. Drain, then toss with the pesto in a large bowl.

5 Add the capsicum pieces, steak slices and mushroom quarters to the penne and toss to distribute evenly. Serve immediately.

NUTRITION PER SERVE
Protein 8 g; Fat 5 g; Carbohydrate 15 g;
Dietary Fibre 2 g; Cholesterol 7 mg;
660 kJ (135 Cal)

When the capsicum has cooled, peel away the skin and dice the flesh.

Cook the steak in a non-stick frying pan until it is medium-rare.

Add the oil with the orange and lemon juice, in a thin stream.

SPAGHETTI, TOMATO AND BASIL SALAD

Preparation time: 25 minutes
Total cooking time: 15 minutes
Serves 4–6

500 g (1 lb) spaghetti
1 cup (30 g/1 oz) fresh basil leaves
250 g (8 oz) cherry tomatoes, halved

1 clove garlic, crushed
1/2 cup (60 g/2 oz) chopped black
  olives
3 tablespoons olive oil
1 tablespoon balsamic vinegar
1/2 cup (60 g/2 oz) grated Parmesan

1 Cook the pasta in a large pan of rapidly boiling salted water until *al dente*. Drain well and rinse under cold water. Using a sharp knife, chop the basil leaves into fine strips.
2 Mix together the basil, tomato, garlic, olives, oil and vinegar. Leave for 15 minutes. Toss with the pasta.
3 Add the Parmesan and some salt and pepper. Toss well to serve.

NUTRITION PER SERVE (6)
Protein 14 g; Fat 15 g; Carbohydrate 65 g;
Dietary Fibre 14 g; Cholesterol 10 mg;
1866 kJ (446 Cal)

Chop the basil leaves just before you are ready to use them as the cut edges turn black.

Mix together the basil, tomato, garlic, olives, oil and vinegar and leave to stand.

After tossing the pasta salad, add the Parmesan and salt and pepper and toss again.

LARB (SPICY THAI PORK SALAD)

Preparation time: 20 minutes
Total cooking time: 8 minutes
Serves 4–6

1 tablespoon oil
2 stems lemon grass, white part only, thinly sliced
2 fresh green chillies, finely chopped
500 g (1 lb) lean pork mince
1/4 cup (60 ml/2 fl oz) lime juice
2 teaspoons finely grated lime rind
2–6 teaspoons chilli sauce
lettuce leaves, for serving
1/3 cup (10 g/1/4 oz) coriander leaves
1/4 cup (5 g/1/4 oz) small mint leaves
1 small onion, very finely sliced
1/3 cup (50 g/1 3/4 oz) roasted unsalted peanuts, chopped
3 tablespoons crisp-fried garlic

1 Heat the oil in a wok. Add the lemon grass, chilli and pork mince. Stir-fry, breaking up any lumps with a fork or wooden spoon, over high heat for 6 minutes, or until cooked through. Transfer to a bowl and allow to cool.
2 Add the lime juice and rind and the chilli sauce to the cooled mince. Arrange the lettuce leaves on a serving plate. Stir most of the coriander and mint leaves, onion, peanuts and fried garlic through the mince. Spoon over the lettuce and sprinkle the rest of the leaves, onion, peanuts and garlic over the top to serve.

NUTRITION PER SERVE (6)
Protein 22 g; Fat 8.5 g; Carbohydrate 3.5 g;
Dietary Fibre 2 g; Cholesterol 40 mg;
760 kJ (180 Cal)

Finely slice the white part of the lemon grass with a sharp knife.

Stir-fry the lemon grass, chilli and mince, breaking up the mince as it cooks.

Add the lime juice, lime rind and chilli sauce to the cooled mince.

FELAFEL WITH TOMATO SALSA

Preparation time: 40 minutes + 4 hours
 soaking + 30 minutes standing
Total cooking time: 20 minutes
Serves 8

2 cups (440 g/14 oz) dried chickpeas
1 small onion, finely chopped
2 cloves garlic, crushed
4 tablespoons chopped fresh flat-leaf
 parsley
2 tablespoons chopped fresh
 coriander leaves
2 teaspoons ground cumin
1/2 teaspoon baking powder
oil, for deep-frying

TOMATO SALSA
2 tomatoes
1/4 Lebanese cucumber, finely
 chopped
1/2 green capsicum, diced
2 tablespoons chopped fresh flat-leaf
 parsley
1 teaspoon sugar
2 teaspoons chilli sauce
1/2 teaspoon grated lemon rind
2 tablespoons lemon juice

1 Soak the chickpeas in 1 litre (32 fl oz) water for 4 hours or overnight. Drain. Place in a food processor and blend for 30 seconds, or until finely ground. Add the onion, garlic, parsley, coriander, cumin, baking powder and 1 tablespoon water, then process for 10 seconds to make a rough paste. Leave, covered, for 30 minutes.
2 To make the salsa, score a cross in the base of each tomato. Put them in a bowl of boiling water for 30 seconds, then plunge into cold water and peel the skin away from the cross. Finely chop, then place in a bowl with all the other ingredients and mix well.
3 Using your hands, shape heaped tablespoons of the felafel mixture into even-sized balls. If there is any excess liquid, squeeze it out. Fill a large heavy-based saucepan one-third full of oil and heat until a cube of bread dropped into the oil browns in 15 seconds.
4 Lower the felafel balls into the oil and cook in batches of five for 3–4 minutes, or until well browned all over. Remove the felafel with a slotted spoon and drain on paper towels. Serve hot or cold on a bed of the tomato salsa, with pitta bread.

NUTRITION PER SERVE
Protein 10.5 g; Fat 8 g; Carbohydrate 22.5 g; Dietary Fibre 8 g; Cholesterol 0 mg; 855 kJ (204 cal)

Grind the drained chickpeas in a food processor until finely chopped.

Shape heaped tablespoons of the felafel mixture into even-sized balls.

Cook until well browned, then remove them with a slotted spoon and drain.

MISO TOFU STICKS WITH CUCUMBER AND WAKAME SALAD

Preparation time: 30 minutes +
 20 minutes standing
Total cooking time: 15 minutes
Serves 4

3 Lebanese cucumbers, thinly sliced
20 g (3/4 oz) dried wakame
500 g (1 lb) silken firm tofu, well
 drained
3 tablespoons shiro miso
1 tablespoon mirin
1 tablespoon sugar
1 tablespoon rice vinegar
1 egg yolk
100 g (3½ oz) bean sprouts,
 blanched
2 tablespoons sesame seeds, toasted

DRESSING
3 tablespoons rice vinegar
¼ teaspoon soy sauce
1½ tablespoons sugar
1 tablespoon mirin

1 Sprinkle the cucumber generously with salt and leave for 20 minutes, or until very soft, then rinse and drain. To rehydrate the wakame, place it in a colander in the sink and leave it under cold running water for 10 minutes, then drain well.
2 Place the tofu in a colander, weigh down with a plate and leave to drain.
3 Place the shiro miso, mirin, sugar, rice vinegar and 2 tablespoons water in a saucepan and stir over low heat for 1 minute, or until the sugar dissolves. Remove from the heat, then add the egg yolk and whisk until glossy. Cool slightly.
4 Cut the tofu into thick sticks and

place on a non-stick baking tray. Brush the miso mixture over the tofu and cook under a hot grill (broiler) for 6 minutes each side, or until light golden on both sides.
5 To make the dressing, place all the ingredients and ½ teaspoon salt in a bowl and whisk together well.
6 To assemble, place the cucumber in

the centre of a plate, top with the sprouts and wakame, drizzle with the dressing, top with tofu and serve sprinkled with the sesame seeds.

NUTRITION PER SERVE
Protein 10 g; Fat 7 g; Carbohydrate 8 g;
Dietary Fibre 2.5 g; Cholesterol 0 mg;
710 kJ (180 Cal)

Once the cucumber is very soft, rinse the salt off under running water.

Place the wakame in a colander and leave it under cold running water.

Brush the miso mixture over the tofu sticks and grill under golden.

ASPARAGUS AND MUSHROOM SALAD

Preparation time: 20 minutes
Total cooking time: 10 minutes
Serves 4

155 g (5 oz) asparagus spears
1 tablespoon wholegrain mustard
1/4 cup (60 ml/2 fl oz) orange juice
2 tablespoons lemon juice
1 tablespoon lime juice
1 tablespoon orange zest
2 teaspoons lemon zest
2 teaspoons lime zest

2 cloves garlic, crushed
1/4 cup (90 g/3 oz) honey
400 g (13 oz) button mushrooms, halved
150 g (5 oz) rocket
1 red capsicum, cut into strips

1 Snap the woody ends from the asparagus spears and cut in half on the diagonal. Cook in boiling water for 1 minute, or until just tender. Drain, plunge into cold water and set aside.
2 Place the mustard, citrus juice and zest, garlic and honey in a large saucepan and season with pepper. Bring to the boil, then reduce the heat and add the mushrooms, tossing for 2 minutes. Cool.
3 Remove the mushrooms from the sauce with a slotted spoon. Return the sauce to the heat, bring to the boil, then reduce the heat and simmer for 3–5 minutes, or until reduced and syrupy. Cool slightly.
4 Toss the mushrooms, rocket leaves, capsicum and asparagus. Put on a plate and drizzle with the sauce.

NUTRITION PER SERVE
Protein 6 g; Fat 0 g; Carbohydrate 25 g;
Dietary Fibre 5 g; Cholesterol 0 mg;
550 kJ (132 cal)

Use a zester to remove the zest of the orange, lemon and lime.

Toss the mushrooms in the mustard, juices, zest, garlic and honey.

Remove the mushrooms and simmer the sauce until it is reduced and syrupy.

VIETNAMESE NOODLE SALAD

Preparation time: 30 minutes +
  10 minutes standing + 30 minutes
  refrigeration
Total cooking time: Nil
Serves 4–6

200 g (6^1/$_2$ oz) dried rice vermicelli
1 cup (140 g/4^1/$_2$ oz) crushed peanuts
^{1}/$_2$ cup (10 g/^{1}/$_4$ oz) fresh Vietnamese
  mint leaves, torn
^{1}/$_2$ cup (15 g/^{1}/$_2$ oz) firmly packed
  fresh coriander leaves
^{1}/$_2$ red onion, cut into thin wedges

1 green mango, cut into julienne strips
1 Lebanese cucumber, halved
  lengthways and thinly sliced on the
  diagonal

LEMON GRASS DRESSING
^{1}/$_2$ cup (125 ml/4 fl oz) lime juice
1 tablespoon shaved palm sugar
^{1}/$_4$ cup (60 ml/2 fl oz) seasoned rice
  vinegar
2 stems lemon grass, finely chopped
2 red chillies, seeded and finely
  chopped
3 kaffir lime leaves, shredded

1 Put the rice vermicelli in a bowl and cover with boiling water. Leave for 10 minutes, or until soft, then drain, rinse under cold water and cut into short lengths.
2 Place the vermicelli, three-quarters of the peanuts, the mint, coriander, onion, mango and cucumber in a large bowl and toss together.
3 To make the dressing, put all the ingredients in a jar with a lid and shake.
4 Toss the salad and dressing and refrigerate for 30 minutes. Sprinkle with the remaining nuts to serve.

NUTRITION PER SERVE (6)
Protein 6.5 g; Fat 13 g; Carbohydrate 19 g;
Dietary Fibre 3 g; Cholesterol 0 mg;
926 kJ (221 Cal)

Cut the green mango into julienne strips (the size and shape of matchsticks).

Using scissors, cut the rice vermicelli into shorter, more manageable lengths.

Put the salad ingredients in a bowl and toss well, reserving some of the peanuts to garnish.

TABBOULEH WITH SOY GRITS AND CHICKPEAS

Preparation time: 20 minutes + soaking
Total cooking time: Nil
Serves 6–8

150 g (5 oz) fresh flat-leaf parsley
1 cup (180 g/6 oz) soy grits
2 tablespoons chopped fresh mint
1 small red onion, cut into thin wedges
3 ripe tomatoes, chopped

400 g (13 oz) can chickpeas, rinsed and drained
3 tablespoons lemon juice
2 tablespoons extra virgin olive oil
Lebanese or pitta bread, to serve

1 Remove all the parsley leaves from the stalks, roughly chop and place in a large serving bowl.
2 Place the soy grits in a heatproof bowl and pour in $2/3$ cup (170 ml/ $15^1/2$ fl oz) boiling water. Leave to soak for 3 minutes, or until all the water has been absorbed.
3 Add the soy grits to the parsley, along with the mint, onion, tomato

and chickpeas. Drizzle with the lemon juice and olive oil. Season well with salt and freshly ground black pepper and toss together.
4 Serve with Lebanese or pitta bread and Soy bean hummus as a vegetarian meal, or as an accompaniment to barbecued meat, chicken or fish.

NUTRITION PER SERVE (8)
Protein 12 g; Fat 11 g; Carbohydrate 13 g; Dietary Fibre 6.5 g; Cholesterol 0 mg; 820 kJ (196 Cal)

Cut the red onion into thin wedges with a sharp knife.

Allow the grits and water to soak until the liquid has been absorbed.

Toss together the grits, parsley, mint, onion, tomato, chickpeas and dressing.

SOMEN NOODLE SALAD WITH SESAME DRESSING

Preparation time: 25 minutes + cooling
Total cooking time: 5 minutes
Serves 4

SESAME DRESSING
1/3 cup (40 g/1 oz) sesame seeds, toasted
2 1/2 tablespoons Japanese or light soy sauce
2 tablespoons rice vinegar
2 teaspoons sugar
1/2 teaspoon grated fresh ginger
1/2 teaspoon dashi granules

125 g (4 oz) dried somen noodles
100 g (3 1/2 oz) snow peas, finely sliced on the diagonal
100 g daikon radish, julienned
1 small (100 g/3 1/2 oz) carrot, julienned
1 spring onion, sliced on the diagonal

60 g (2 oz) baby English spinach leaves, trimmed
2 teaspoons toasted sesame seeds

1 To make the dressing, place the sesame seeds in a mortar and pestle and grind until fine and moist. Combine the soy sauce, rice vinegar, sugar, ginger, dashi granules and 1/2 cup (125 ml/4 fl oz) water in a small saucepan and bring to the boil over high heat. Reduce the heat to medium and simmer, stirring, for 2 minutes, or until the dashi granules have dissolved. Remove from the heat. Cool. Gradually combine with the ground sesame seeds, stirring to form a thick dressing.
2 Cook the noodles in a large saucepan of boiling water for 2 minutes, or until tender. Drain, rinse under cold water and cool completely. Cut into 10 cm (4 inch) lengths using scissors.
3 Place the snow peas in a large

shallow bowl with the daikon, carrot, spring onion, English spinach leaves and the noodles. Add the dressing and toss well to combine. Place in the refrigerator until ready to serve. Just before serving, sprinkle the top with the toasted sesame seeds.

NUTRITION PER SERVE
Protein 8 g; Fat 7.5 g; Carbohydrate 27 g; Dietary Fibre 4 g; Cholesterol 0.5 mg; 885 kJ (210 Cal)

Pour the soy sauce mixture into the sesame seeds, stirring to form a thick dressing.

PORK NOODLE SALAD

Preparation time: 20 minutes +
  10 minutes soaking
Cooking time: 35 minutes
Serves 4–6

ASIAN BROTH
1 cup (250 ml/8 fl oz) chicken
   stock
3 coriander roots
2 kaffir lime leaves
3 cm x 3 cm (1¼ inch x 1¼ inch)
   piece ginger, sliced

30 g (1 oz) fresh black fungus
100 g (3½ oz) dried rice vermicelli
1 small red chilli, seeded and
   finely sliced
2 red Asian shallots, thinly sliced
2 spring onions, thinly sliced
2 cloves garlic, crushed
250 g (8 oz) minced (ground) pork
3 tablespoons lime juice
3 tablespoons fish sauce
1½ tablespoons grated palm sugar
¼ teaspoon ground white pepper
15 g (½ cup) coriander leaves,
   chopped
oakleaf or coral lettuce, to serve
lime wedges, to garnish

long red chilli, seeded and cut into
   strips, to garnish
coriander (cilantro) leaves, extra,
   to garnish (optional)

1 To make the Asian broth, place the stock, coriander roots, lime leaves, ginger and 1 cup (250 ml/8 fl oz) water in a saucepan. Simmer for 25 minutes, or until liquid has reduced to ¾ cup (185 ml/6 fl oz). Strain and return to the pan.
2 Discard the woody stems from the fungus, then thinly slice. Soak the vermicelli in boiling water for 6–7 minutes. Drain, then cut into 3 cm (1¼ inch) lengths. Combine the vermicelli, fungus, chilli, red Asian shallots, spring onion and garlic.
3 Return the stock to the heat and

bring to the boil. Add the minced pork and stir, breaking up any lumps, for 1–2 minutes, or until the pork changes colour and is cooked. Drain, then add to the vermicelli mixture.
4 sauce, palm sugar and white pepper, stirring until the sugar has dissolved. Add to the pork mixture with the coriander and mix well. Season with salt.
5 To assemble, tear or shred the lettuce, then arrange on a serving dish. Spoon on the pork and noodle mixture and garnish with the lime wedges, chilli and extra coriander.

NUTRITION PER SERVE (6)
Protein 11 g; Fat 3.5 g; Carbohydrate 15.5 g;
Dietary Fibre 1.5 g; Cholesterol 26.5 mg;
580 kJ (140 Cal)

Cut, then discard the woody ends from the fresh black fungus.

Add the cooked minced pork to the noodles and salad ingredients.

VEGETABLE AND SCALLOP SALAD

Preparation time: 40 minutes
Total cooking time: 15 minutes
Serves 4–6

1/4 red cabbage
1 carrot
2 celery sticks
1 red capsicum
1 green capsicum
1 yellow capsicum
100 g (3¼ oz) snow peas
300 g (10 oz) scallops
1 tablespoon black sesame
   seeds

DRESSING
grated rind of 1 lime
90 ml (3 fl oz) lime juice
2 tablespoons fish sauce
1 tablespoon grated palm sugar
1 small red chilli, finely chopped
1/2 teaspoon sesame oil

1 Finely shred the red cabbage. Cut the carrot, celery, capsicums and snow peas into julienne strips, the size and shape of matchsticks.
2 Chargrill the scallops in batches on a lightly oiled chargrill pan or barbecue hotplate until they are tender.
3 To make the dressing, put the lime rind and juice, fish sauce, sugar, chilli and oil in a small bowl. Whisk gently to combine.
4 Combine the chopped vegetables, chargrilled scallops and sesame seeds in a large bowl. Pour in the dressing and toss to coat.

NUTRITION PER SERVE (6)
Protein 10 g; Fat 2 g; Carbohydrate 8 g;
Dietary Fibre 6 g; Cholesterol 15 mg;
405 kJ (95 Cal)

NOTE: Black sesame seeds are available from Asian food stores. If they are not available, they may be substituted with white sesame seeds.

Using the coarse side of a metal grater, grate the palm sugar.

Cut the carrot, celery and capsicums into julienne strips.

Chargrill the scallops in batches until they are tender.

Vinaigrettes & Dressings

BASIC VINAIGRETTE (FRENCH DRESSING)

Combine 1/2 cup (125 ml/4 fl oz) extra virgin olive oil,
2 tablespoons white wine vinegar and 1 teaspoon sugar in a
small jug. Whisk with a small wire whisk or fork until well
blended, and season with salt and freshly ground black
pepper. Makes about 2/3 cup (170 ml/51/2 fl oz)

NUTRITION PER 100 G: Protein 0 g; Fat 70 g; Carbohydrate 2 g; Dietary
Fibre 0 g; Cholesterol 0 mg; 2600 kJ (620 Cal)

LEMON SOY DRESSING

Put 2 tablespoons soy sauce, 2 tablespoons rice wine
vinegar, 1 teaspoon honey, 2 tablespoons lemon juice and
1 teaspoon finely grated lemon rind in a small jug. Gradually
whisk in 1/3 cup (80 ml/23/4 fl oz) vegetable oil in a thin
stream until well blended. Season with freshly ground black
pepper. Makes about 3/4 cup (185 ml/6 fl oz)

NUTRITION PER 100 G: Protein 1 g; Fat 35 g; Carbohydrate 4 g; Dietary
Fibre 0 g; Cholesterol 0 mg; 1430 kJ (340 Cal)

BASIL GARLIC DRESSING

Process 1 clove garlic and 2 tablespoons chopped basil in a
food processor or blender until finely chopped. Add 1/4 cup
(60 ml/2 fl oz) lemon juice and process in short bursts until
combined. Gradually add 1/2 cup (125 ml/4 fl oz) extra virgin
olive oil and process until combined. Season with salt and
ground black pepper. Makes about 3/4 cup (185 ml/6 fl oz)

NUTRITION PER 100 G: Protein 0 g; Fat 60 g; Carbohydrate 1 g; Dietary
Fibre 1 g; Cholesterol 0 mg; 2335 kJ (555 Cal)

BLUE CHEESE DRESSING

Mash 80 g (23/4 oz) blue cheese with a fork to a chunky paste.
Add 1/2 cup (125 g/4 oz) whole egg mayonnaise, 1/4 cup
(60 g/2 oz) sour cream, and freshly ground white pepper to
taste. Stir in 1 tablespoon chopped chives and 1 teaspoon
white wine vinegar. Makes about 11/4 cups (315 ml/10 fl oz)

NUTRITION PER 100 G: Protein 7 g; Fat 35 g; Carbohydrate 10 g; Dietary
Fibre 0 g; Cholesterol 70 mg; 1495 kJ (355 Cal)

Top row: Basic Vinaigrette; Basil Garlic Dressing; Ginger and Sesame Dressing; Balsamic Dressing
Bottom row: Lemon Soy Dressing; Blue Cheese Dressing; Chilli Lime Dressing; Thousand Island Dressing

GINGER AND SESAME DRESSING

Put 1 teaspoon sesame oil, 3 teaspoons rice wine vinegar, 1 teaspoon finely grated orange rind, 2 tablespoons orange juice and 2 teaspoons grated fresh ginger in a small jug. Gradually whisk in 1/2 cup (125 ml/4 fl oz) vegetable oil until well blended. Season with salt and freshly ground black pepper. Makes about 3/4 cup (185 ml/6 fl oz)

NUTRITION PER 100 G: Protein 0 g; Fat 65 g; Carbohydrate 2 g; Dietary Fibre 0 g; Cholesterol 0 mg; 2460 kJ (585 Cal)

CHILLI LIME DRESSING

Put 1/4 cup (60 ml/2 fl oz) lime juice, 2 tablespoons fish sauce, 1–2 teaspoons sambal oelek and 1 teaspoon sugar in a small jug. Using a small wire whisk or fork, gradually whisk in 1/4 cup (60 ml/2 fl oz) vegetable oil in a thin stream until well blended. Makes about 3/4 cup (185 ml/6 fl oz)

NUTRITION PER 100 G: Protein 2 g; Fat 35 g; Carbohydrate 4 g; Dietary Fibre 0 g; Cholesterol 0 mg; 1365 kJ (325 Cal)

BALSAMIC DRESSING

Whisk 2 tablespoons balsamic vinegar and 1 teaspoon French mustard in a small jug until combined. Gradually beat in 1/3 cup (80 ml/2 3/4 fl oz) extra virgin olive oil. Season with salt and freshly ground black pepper. Cut 1 small clove garlic in half, skewer onto a toothpick and leave in the dressing to infuse for at least 1 hour. Makes about 1/2 cup (125 ml/4 fl oz)

NUTRITION PER 100 G: Protein 0 g; Fat 55 g; Carbohydrate 0 g; Dietary Fibre 1 g; Cholesterol 0 mg; 2145 kJ (510 Cal)

THOUSAND ISLAND DRESSING

Put 1/2 cup whole egg mayonnaise, 1 tablespoon tomato paste, 1 teaspoon Worcestershire sauce, 1 teaspoon French mustard and 2 teaspoons chilli sauce in a small bowl and stir until well combined. Season with salt. Makes about 1/2 cup (125 ml/4 fl oz)

NUTRITION PER 100 G: Protein 1 g; Fat 25 g; Carbohydrate 20 g; Dietary Fibre 1 g; Cholesterol 25 mg; 1265 kJ (300 Cal)

Mayonnaises

BASIC MAYONNAISE
Place 2 egg yolks, 2 teaspoons Dijon mustard and
2 teaspoons lemon juice in a food processor or blender and
process for 30 seconds, or until light and creamy. Add 1 cup
(250 ml/8 fl oz) olive oil in a thin, steady stream, increasing
the flow as the mayonnaise thickens. Stir in 2–4 teaspoons
lemon juice and season with salt and freshly ground white
pepper. Makes about $1^1/4$ cups (310 g/10 oz)
NUTRITION PER 100 G: Protein 2 g; Fat 80 g; Carbohydrate 0 g; Dietary
Fibre 0 g; Cholesterol 115 mg; 3040 kJ (725 Cal)

GARLIC MAYONNAISE
Place 2 egg yolks, 2 teaspoons lemon juice and 2 crushed
cloves garlic in a food processor or blender and process for
30 seconds, or until light and creamy. Gradually add 1 cup
(250 ml/8 fl oz) olive oil in a thin stream. Increase the
amount of oil added as the mayonnaise thickens. Stir in
2 teaspoons lemon juice and season with salt and freshly

ground black pepper. Makes about $1^1/4$ cups (310 g/10 oz)
NUTRITION PER 100 G: Protein 2 g; Fat 85 g; Carbohydrate 0 g; Dietary
Fibre 0 g; Cholesterol 120 mg; 3110 kJ (740 Cal)

MUSTARD MAYONNAISE
Place 2 egg yolks, 2 teaspoons white wine vinegar,
2 teaspoons Dijon mustard and 2 tablespoons wholegrain
mustard in a food processor or blender and process for
30 seconds, or until light and creamy. Gradually add 1 cup
(250 ml/8 fl oz) olive oil in a thin stream. Increase the
amount of oil added as the mayonnaise thickens. Stir in
2 teaspoons white wine vinegar, $1/2$ teaspoon honey and
1 tablespoon chopped tarragon (optional). Season with salt
and freshly ground white pepper. Makes about $1^1/3$ cups
(340 g/$10^3/4$ oz)
NUTRITION PER 100 G: Protein 2 g; Fat 70 g; Carbohydrate 2 g; Dietary
Fibre 1 g; Cholesterol 100 mg; 2705 kJ (645 Cal)

Top row: Basic Mayonnaise; Mustard Mayonnaise (large picture); Spicy Mayonnaise; Green Goddess Dressing
Bottom row: Garlic Mayonnaise; Lime and Yoghurt Mayonnaise; Roasted Red Capsicum Mayonnaise

SPICY MAYONNAISE

Process 2 egg yolks and 2 teaspoons lime juice in a food processor or blender for 30 seconds, or until light and creamy. Gradually add 1 cup (250 ml/8 fl oz) olive oil in a thin stream. Increase the amount of oil added as the mayonnaise thickens. Stir in 1/4 teaspoon chilli flakes, 1/4 cup (15 g/1/2 oz) chopped coriander, 1 teaspoon grated fresh ginger and 1 tablespoon lime juice. Season with salt. Makes about 11/4 cups (310 g/10 oz)

NUTRITION PER 100 G: Protein 2 g; Fat 75 g; Carbohydrate 0 g; Dietary Fibre 0 g; Cholesterol 110 mg; 2895 kJ (690 Cal)

LIME AND YOGHURT MAYONNAISE

Combine 1/2 cup (125 g/4 oz) each of ready-made whole egg mayonnaise and plain yoghurt. Mix in the rind and juice of 1 lime. Makes 1 cup (250 g/8 oz)

NUTRITION PER 100 G: Protein 2 g; Fat 15 g; Carbohydrate 9 g; Dietary Fibre 1 g; Cholesterol 15 mg; 690 kJ (165 Cal)

GREEN GODDESS DRESSING

To 1 quantity of the basic mayonnaise add 4 finely chopped anchovy fillets, 1 crushed clove garlic, 1/4 cup (60 g/2 oz) sour cream and 1/4 cup (15 g/1/2 oz) chopped fresh herbs. Makes about 13/4 cups (435 g/133/4 oz)

NUTRITION PER 100 G: Protein 3 g; Fat 60 g; Carbohydrate 2 g; Dietary Fibre 2 g; Cholesterol 100 mg; 2325 kJ (555 Cal)

ROASTED RED CAPSICUM MAYONNAISE

Cut 2 red capsicums into large pieces, removing the seeds and membrane. Place, skin-side-up, under a hot grill until the skin blackens and blisters. Cool in a plastic bag, then peel away the skin. Chop the flesh very finely and combine with 1/2 cup (125 g/4 oz) ready-made whole egg mayonnaise and 1 crushed clove garlic. Season with salt and black pepper. Makes about 2/3 cup (160 g/51/4 oz)

NUTRITION PER 100 G: Protein 1 g; Fat 10 g; Carbohydrate 9 g; Dietary Fibre 1 g; Cholesterol 10 mg; 550 kJ (130 Cal)

Glossary

Anchovies are a small fish from the herring family found mainly in southern European waters. Although they can be eaten fresh, they are rarely found outside Mediterranean fishing ports. More commonly, they are cured and packed in oil, salt or brine and are readily available in cans or jars.

Balsamic vinegar is a rich, sweet and fragrant vinegar originating from Modena in Italy. Often used in dressings.

Besan (chickpea flour)

Bocconcini are small balls of fresh Italian mozzarella available from delicatessens. Keep refrigerated and covered in the whey in which they are sold for up to 3 weeks. Discard if they show signs of yellowing.

Butter beans (lima beans)

Calamari (squid)

Capers are the pickled buds of a shrub that grows wild in many parts of the Mediterranean. Capers have a sharp, sour taste and are sold in seasoned vinegar or packed in salt which needs to be rinsed off before use.

Clams (vongole)

Cannellini beans (white beans, Italian white beans) are available canned or dried.

Capsicum (pepper)

Caster sugar (superfine sugar) is a fine white sugar with very small crystals.

Coconut cream and milk are extracted from the flesh of fresh coconuts. The cream is thick and almost spreadable. The milk is extracted after the cream has been pressed and is thinner.

Eggplants (aubergines) come in a variety of shapes, sizes and colours. Slender eggplants are also called baby, finger or Japanese eggplants, while the most commonly used are larger and rounder.

Feta cheese is a soft, fresh goat's or ewe's milk cheese ripened in brine. It tastes sharp and salty.

Fish sauce is a brown, salty sauce with a characteristic 'fishy' smell. It is made from small fish that have been fermented in the sun. It is a popular seasoning in Southeast Asian cuisine. Use it sparingly as it has a strong flavour.

Green beans (French beans, string beans)

Haloumi is a salty Middle Eastern cheese made from ewe's milk. The curd is cooked, then matured in brine, often with herbs or spices.

Kaffir lime leaves (makrut lime leaves)

Kecap manis is a thick, sweet soy sauce. If unavailable, use regular soy sauce sweetened with a little soft brown sugar.

Lebanese cucumber (short cucumber)

Mirin is a sweetened rice wine and is available from Asian food stores. There is no real substitute.

Nori is dried seaweed that comes in sheets, either plain or roasted. Quick toasting over a naked flame freshens the nori and produces a nutty flavour.

Olive oil comes in different varieties suitable for different purposes. Extra virgin or virgin olive oil are most commonly used in dressings. Regular olive oils are preferred for cooking because of their neutral flavour. Light olive oil refers to the low content of extra virgin olive oil rather than lightness of calories.

Parmesan is a hard cow's milk cheese used widely in Italian cooking. Sold either grated or in blocks, freshly grated has a much better flavour.

Pecorino cheese is a hard sheep's milk cheese. You can substitute Parmesan.

Plain flour (all-purpose flour)

Prawns (shrimp) are crustaceans which come in various sizes and colours. They become opaque and turn pink once cooked.

Prosciutto is an Italian ham that has been cured by salting then drying in the air. Aged for up to ten months, it is then sliced thinly. It does not require cooking. Prosciutto di Parma is the classic Italian ham traditionally served as an antipasto and also used extensively in cooking.

Red Asian shallots are small reddish-purple onions that grow in bulbs like garlic. They are sold in segments that look like large cloves of garlic. They have a concentrated flavour and are easy to slice and grind. If not available, use French shallots or brown or red onions.

Rice vinegar is a clear, pale yellow, mild and sweet-tasting vinegar made from fermented rice.

Roma tomatoes (egg tomatoes, plum tomatoes) are favoured for canning and drying because they have few seeds and a dry flesh. Ideal in sauces and purées. Sometimes called Italian tomatoes.

Semi-dried tomatoes (sun-blushed tomatoes)

Shiitake mushrooms are Asian mushrooms with a dark brown top. Available fresh or dried from supermarkets or Asian food stores.

Snake beans (long beans, yard-long beans) have a crunchy texture and taste similar to green beans. They grow to at least 38 cm (15 inches) long, hence the name. Stringless green beans can be used instead.

Snow peas (mangetout) are a variety of garden pea, eaten whole after being topped and tailed.

Spring onion (scallion, shallot). These immature onions have a mild, delicate flavour, and both the green tops and the white bulbs can be eaten raw or cooked.

Tamari is a naturally brewed, thick Japanese soy sauce; some varieties are wheat-free.

Tahini is a thick oily paste derived from ground sesame seeds. It adds a strong nutty flavour.

Tofu (bean curd) is an excellent source of protein. It comes in varying consistencies, each suitable for different cooking methods (follow the recipe). Fresh tofu doesn't have much taste but absorbs flavours from the food it is cooked with.

Wasabi paste has a pungent taste similar to horseradish.

Zucchini (courgette)

Index

A

Almond and raspberry dressing, 131
anchovy pasta salad, Grilled capsicum and, 123
Asian chicken salad, 136
Asparagus and mushroom salad, 142
Asparagus and red capsicum salad, 48
asparagus pasta salad, Chicken and, 99
avocado and bacon pasta salad, Tomato, 31

B

bacon pasta salad, Tomato, avocado and, 31
Balsamic dressing, 149
Balsamic syrup, 77
Basic mayonnaise, 150
Basic vinaigrette, 148
basil dressing, Smoked tuna and white bean salad with, 86
basil dressing, Summer salad with, 127
Basil garlic dressing, 148
basil salad, Spaghetti, tomato and, 138
basil salad, Vermicelli, beef and Thai, 112
bean and potato salad, Lamb cutlets with beetroot, 98
Bean salad, 37
bean salad, Seared tuna, potato and, 108–9
bean salad with basil dressing, Smoked tuna and white, 86
bean salad with cumin and coriander dressing, Pasta and, 82
Beef and glass noodle salad, 100
beef and noodle salad, Quick, 69
beef and Thai basil salad, Vermicelli, 112
beef salad, Pesto, 137
beef salad with mint and coriander, Thai, 22
beetroot and goat's cheese salad, Fresh, 18–19
beetroot, bean and potato salad, Lamb cutlets with, 98
black olive dressing, Mediterranean pasta salad with, 107
Blue cheese dressing, 148
bread salad, Lebanese toasted, 32

C

cabbage salad, Vietnamese chicken and, 33
Caesar salad, 14
caesar salad, Smoked chicken, 66–7
calamari and parsley salad, Deep-fried, 44
camembert salad, Salmon, leek and, 93
cannellini beans, Chicken salad with rocket and, 95
caper salad, Leek and, 63
capsicum and anchovy pasta salad, Grilled, 123
capsicum mayonnaise, Roasted red, 151
capsicum, pesto and goat's milk cheese salad stack, Eggplant, 61
capsicum salad, Asparagus and red, 48
Caramelized onion and potato salad, 27
cellophane noodle salad, Chilli salt squid and, 74–5
Chargrilled baby octopus salad, 30
Chargrilled chicken salad, 120
Chargrilled tuna and ruby grapefruit salad, 131
Chicken and asparagus pasta salad, 99
chicken and cabbage salad, Vietnamese, 33
chicken and green tea noodle salad, Soy, 111
chicken and noodle salad, Sichuan, 91
Chicken and sesame noodle salad, 85
Chicken and watercress salad, 89
chicken caesar salad, Smoked, 66–7
Chicken citrus salad with curry dressing, 101
chicken, Coronation, 23
Chicken, prawn and grapefruit salad, 117
chicken salad, Asian, 136
chicken salad, Chargrilled, 120
chicken salad, Chilli salt, 105
chicken salad, Pacific, 87
chicken salad, Red curry, 76
chicken salad, Tandoori, 68
chicken salad, Vietnamese pawpaw and, 122
Chicken salad with mustard dressing, 79
Chicken salad with rocket and cannellini beans, 95
chickpea and silverbeet salad with sumac, Warm, 60
Chickpea salad with tahini dressing, 135
chickpeas, Tabbouleh with soy grits and, 144
Chilli lime dressing, 149
Chilli salt chicken salad, 105
Chilli salt squid and cellophane noodle salad, 74–5
Chinese roast duck, lime, herb and noodle salad, 110
citrus salad with curry dressing, Chicken, 101
citrus scallop salad, Sweet, 78
Coconut prawn salad 51
cooking vegetables, 9
coriander dressing, Pasta and bean salad with cumin and, 82
coriander noodle salad, Warm tuna and, 119
coriander, Thai beef salad with mint and, 22
Coronation chicken, 23
couscous salad, Indian-style lamb, 134
Crab, mango and pasta salad, 46–7
cucumber and wakame salad, Miso tofu sticks with, 141
Cucumber and yoghurt dressing, 68
cumin and coriander dressing, Pasta and bean salad with, 82
Curly endive salad with crisp prosciutto and garlic croutons, 29
curry chicken salad, Red, 76
curry dressing, Chicken citrus salad with, 101

D

Deep-fried calamari and parsley salad, 44
dressings and vinaigrettes, 148–9
duck, lime, herb and noodle salad, Chinese roast, 110

E

egg noodle salad, Sesame tuna and, 96
Eggplant, capsicum, pesto and goat's milk cheese salad stack, 61
endive salad with crisp prosciutto and garlic croutons, Curly, 29

F

Farfalle salad with sun-dried tomatoes and spinach, 124–5
Fattoush, 32
Felafel with tomato salsa, 140
fennel and orange salad, Roasted, 57
fennel and rocket salad, Lemon, 41
feta salad, Herbed, 49
freezing vegetables, 8
French dressing, 148
Fresh beetroot and goat's cheese salad, 18–19

G

Gado gado, 28
garlic croutons, Curly endive salad with crisp prosciutto and, 29
garlic dressing, Basil, 148
Garlic mayonnaise, 150
Ginger and sesame dressing, 149
ginger dressing, Tuna and soy bean salad with, 90
ginger miso dressing, Tofu salad with, 121
glass noodle salad, Beef and, 100
goat's cheese salad, Fresh beetroot and, 18–19

goat's milk cheese salad stack, Eggplant, capsicum, pesto and, 61
grapefruit salad, Chargrilled tuna and ruby, 131
grapefruit salad, Chicken, prawn and, 117
Greek pasta salad, 102
Greek salad, 26
Green goddess dressing, 151
green mango salad, Thai-spiced pork and, 116
green peppercorn salad, Scallops and, 126
green tea noodle salad, Soy chicken and, 111
Grilled capsicum and anchovy pasta salad, 123
Guacamole, 55

H
haloumi and spinach salad, Tomato, 50
herb dressing, Squid and scallops with, 88
Herbed feta salad, 49
herbs, salad, 11
Hokkien noodle salad, 20
horseradish cream, Smoked salmon salad with potato rosti and, 40
Hot potato salad, 35

I–K
Indian-style lamb couscous salad, 134
Insalata di fruitti di mare, 70–1
Italian salad, Warm, 83
kaffir lime, Prawn salad with, 129

L
lamb couscous salad, Indian-style, 134
Lamb cutlets with beetroot, bean and potato salad, 98
lamb salad, Tandoori, 118
lamb salad, Warm, 72
Larb, 139
Layered seafood salad, 106
Lebanese toasted bread salad, 32
leek and camembert salad, Salmon, 93
Leek and caper salad, 63

Lemon, fennel and rocket salad, 41
lemon grass dressing, 143
Lemon soy dressing, 148
lentil salad, Spicy, 130
Lime and yoghurt mayonnaise, 151
lime dressing, Chilli, 149
lime, herb and noodle salad, Chinese roast duck, 110
lime, Prawn salad with kaffir, 129
lime vinaigrette, Pear and walnut salad with, 59

M
mango and pasta salad, Crab, 46–7
mango noodle salad, Prawn and, 97
mango salad, Thai-spiced pork and green, 116
Marinated grilled vegetable salad, 42–3
mayonnaises, 150–1
Mediterranean pasta salad with black olive dressing, 107
Mexicana salad, 54–5
mint and coriander, Thai beef salad with, 22
Mint and yoghurt dressing, 130
Mint dressing, 72
minted chicken pasta salad, Warm, 81
Miso tofu sticks with cucumber and wakame salad, 141
mushroom salad, Asparagus and, 142
mushroom salad, Stuffed, 45
mushroom salad, Warm marinated, 56
mushroom salad, Wild, 62
mussel and potato salad, Warm, 113
Mussel salad with saffron dressing, 46–7
mustard dressing, Chicken salad with, 79
Mustard mayonnaise, 150
Mustard vinaigrette, 37

N
noodle salad, Chinese roast duck, lime, herb and, 110
noodle salad, Hokkien, 20
noodle salad, Pork, 146
noodle salad, Prawn, 80
noodle salad, Prawn and mango, 97
noodle salad, Quick beef and, 69
noodle salad, Sichun chicken and, 91
noodle salad, Soy chicken and green tea, 111
noodle salad, Spicy fun see, 133
noodle salad, Vietnamese, 143
noodle salad, Warm tuna and coriander, 119
noodle salad with sesame dressing, Somen, 145

O
octopus salad, Chargrilled baby, 30
olive dressing, Mediterranean pasta salad with black, 107
olive pasta salad, Tuna and, 84
onion and potato salad, Caramelized, 27
orange salad, Roasted fennel and, 57

P
Pacific chicken salad, 87
parsley salad, Deep-fried calamari and 44
Pasta and bean salad with cumin and coriander dressing, 82
pasta salad, Chicken and asparagus, 99
pasta salad, Crab, mango and, 46–7
pasta salad, Greek, 102
pasta salad, Grilled capsicum and anchovy, 123
pasta salad, Prawn and, 73
pasta salad, Salami, 94
pasta salad, Tomato, avocado and bacon, 31
pasta salad, Tuna and olive, 84
pasta salad, Warm minted chicken, 81

pasta salad, Warm pesto, 25
pasta salad, Warm sweet potato, walnut and, 92
pasta salad with black olive dressing, Mediterranean, 107
pasta salad with Thai-style vegetables, Tomato, 132
pasta wrap, Salad, 77
paw paw and chicken salad, Vietnamese, 122
Peanut sauce, 28
Pear and walnut salad with lime vinaigrette, 59
peppercorn salad, Scallops and green, 126
pesto and goat's milk cheese salad stack, Eggplant, capsicum, 61
pesto and prawn salad, Warm, 103
Pesto beef salad, 137
pesto pasta salad, Warm, 25
pork and green mango salad, Thai-spiced, 116
Pork noodle salad, 146
pork salad, Spicy Thai, 139
potato and bean salad, Seared tuna, 108–9
potato rosti and horseradish cream, Smoked salmon salad with, 40
Potato salad, 15
potato salad, Caramelized onion and, 27
potato salad, Hot, 35
potato salad, Lamb cutlets with beetroot, bean and, 98
potato salad, Warm mussel and, 113
prawn and grapefruit salad, Chicken, 117
Prawn and mango noodle salad, 97
Prawn and pasta salad, 73
Prawn cocktails, 17
Prawn noodle salad, 80
prawn salad, Warm pesto and, 103
prawn salad, Coconut, 51
Prawn salad with kaffir lime, 129
preparing vegetables, 8–9

prosciutto and garlic croutons, Curly endive salad with crisp, 29
purchasing vegetables, 6–7

Q–R

Quick beef and noodle salad, 69
Red curry chicken salad, 76
Rice salad, 34
Roasted fennel and orange salad, 57
Roasted red capsicum mayonnaise, 151
rocket and cannellini beans, Chicken salad with, 95
rocket salad, Lemon, fennel and, 41
rocket salad, Smoked salmon and, 52

S

saffron dressing, Mussel salad with, 46–7
salad greens, 10–11
Salad nicoise, 16
Salad pasta wrap, 77
Salami pasta salad, 94
salmon and avocado salad, Soba, 104
salmon and rocket salad, Smoked, 52
Salmon, leek and camembert salad, 93
salmon salad with potato rosti and horseradish cream, Smoked, 40
Salt-and-pepper squid salad, 128
Sashimi timbales, 58
scallop salad, Sweet citrus, 78
scallop salad, Vegetable and, 147
Scallops and green peppercorn salad, 126
scallops with herb dressing, Squid and, 88
Seafood salad, 70–1
seafood salad, Layered, 106
Seared tuna, potato and bean salad, 108–9
Sesame dressing, 20
sesame dressing, Ginger and, 149
sesame dressing, Somen noodle salad with, 145

sesame dressing, Toasted, 41
sesame noodle salad, Chicken and, 85
Sesame tuna and egg noodle salad, 96
Sichuan chicken and noodle salad, 91
silverbeet salad with sumac, Warm chickpea and, 60
Smoked chicken caesar salad, 66–7
Smoked salmon and rocket salad, 52
Smoked salmon salad with potato rosti and horseradish cream, 40
Smoked tuna and white bean salad with basil dressing, 86
Snow pea salad, 53
Soba, salmon and avocado salad, 104
Somen noodle salad with sesame dressing, 145
soy bean salad with ginger dressing, Tuna and, 90
Soy chicken and green tea noodle salad, 111
soy grits and chickpeas, Tabbouleh with, 144
Spaghetti, tomato and basil salad, 138
Spicy fun see noodle salad, 133
Spicy lentil salad, 130
Spicy mayonnaise, 151
Spicy Thai pork salad, 139
spinach, Farfalle salad with sun-dried tomatoes and, 124–5
Spinach salad, 36
spinach salad, Tomato, haloumi and, 50
squid and cellophane noodle salad, Chilli salt, 74–5
Squid and scallops with herb dressing, 88
squid salad, Salt-and-pepper, 128
storing vegetables, 7–8
Stuffed mushroom salad, 45
sumac, Warm chickpea and silverbeet salad with, 60
Summer salad with basil dressing, 127

sun-dried tomatoes and spinach, Farfalle salad with, 124–5
Sweet citrus scallop salad, 78
sweet potato, walnut and pasta salad, Warm, 92

T

Tabbouleh, 21
Tabbouleh with soy grits and chickpeas, 144
tahini dressing, Chickpea salad with, 135
Tandoori chicken salad, 68
Tandoori lamb salad, 118
Thai basil salad, Vermicelli, beef and, 112
Thai beef salad with mint and coriander, 22
Thai pork salad, Spicy, 139
Thai-spiced pork and green mango salad, 116
Thai-style vegetables, Tomato pasta salad with, 132
Thousand Island dressing, 149
Toasted sesame dressing, 41
Tofu salad with ginger miso dressing, 121
tofu sticks with cucumber and wakame salad, Miso, 141
tomato and basil salad, Spaghetti, 138
Tomato, avocado and bacon pasta salad, 31
Tomato, haloumi and spinach salad, 50
Tomato mustard vinaigrette, 62
Tomato pasta salad with Thai-style vegetables, 132
tomato salsa, Felafel with, 140
tomatoes and spinach, Farfalle salad with sun-dried, 124–5
tuna and coriander noodle salad, Warm, 119
tuna and egg noodle salad, Sesame, 96
Tuna and olive pasta salad, 84
tuna and ruby grapefruit salad, Chargrilled, 131
Tuna and soy bean salad with ginger dressing, 90
tuna and white bean salad with basil dressing, Smoked, 86

tuna, potato and bean salad, Seared, 108–9

V

Vegetable and scallop salad, 147
vegetable basics, 6–9
vegetable juices, 9
vegetable salad, Marinated grilled, 42–3
Vermicelli, beef and Thai basil salad, 112
Vietnamese chicken and cabbage salad, 33
Vietnamese noodle salad, 143
Vietnamese pawpaw and chicken salad, 122
vinaigrettes and dressings, 148–9

W–Y

wakame salad, Miso tofu sticks with cucumber and, 141
Waldorf salad, 24
walnut and pasta salad, Warm sweet potato, 92
walnut salad with lime vinaigrette, Pear and, 59
Warm chickpea and silverbeet salad with sumac, 60
Warm Italian salad, 83
Warm lamb salad, 72
Warm marinated mushroom salad, 56
Warm minted chicken pasta salad, 81
Warm mussel and potato salad, 113
Warm pesto and prawn salad, 103
Warm pesto pasta salad, 25
Warm sweet potato, walnut and pasta salad, 92
Warm tuna and coriander noodle salad, 119
Wasabi mayonnaise, 58
watercress salad, Chicken and, 89
Wild mushroom salad, 62
yoghurt mayonnaise, Lime and, 151

Published by Murdoch Books®, a division of Murdoch Magazines Pty Ltd.

Murdoch Books® Australia
Pier 8/9, 23 Hickson Road
Millers Point NSW 2000
Phone: + 61 (0) 2 4352 7000
Fax: + 61 (0) 2 4352 7026

Murdoch Books UK Limited
Erico House
6th Floor North
93–99 Upper Richmond Road
Putney, London SW15 2TG
Phone: + 44 (0) 20 8785 5995
Fax: + 44 (0) 20 8785 5985

Editorial Director: Diana Hill
Project Manager: Zoë Harpham
Editor: Stephanie Kistner
Creative Director: Marylouise Brammer
Designer: Annette Fitzgerald
Production: Monika Paratore
Recipes developed by the Murdoch Books Test Kitchen.

Chief Executive: Juliet Rogers
Publisher: Kay Scarlett

The Publisher gratefully acknowledges the contribution of the recipe writers, chefs,
photographers and stylists who worked on the material appearing in this publication.

National Library of Australia Cataloguing-in-Publication Data
Everyday salads. Includes index. ISBN 1 74045 206 2.
1. Salads. 2. Cookery. (Series: Everyday series (Sydney, NSW)).
641.83

PRINTED IN CHINA by Toppan Printing Co. (HK) Ltd.
Printed 2004.

IMPORTANT: Those who might be at risk from the effects of salmonella food poisoning
(the elderly, pregnant women, young children and those suffering from immune deficiency diseases)
should consult their doctor with any concerns about eating raw eggs.